The Ancient Egyptians
Their Lives and Their World

Angela McDonald

THE BRITISH MUSEUM PRESS

© 2008 Angela McDonald

Published in 2008 by British Museum Press
A division of The British Museum Company Ltd
38 Russell Square, London WC1B 3QQ

ISBN 978-0-7141-3115-3

Angela McDonald has asserted her right to be
identified as the author of this work.

A catalogue record for this title is available
from the British Library.

Designed and typeset by John Hawkins
Printed in China by C&C Offset Printing Co. Ltd

Illustration Acknowledgements
Unless otherwise noted below, the photographs in this book
show objects from the collections of the British Museum.
They were taken by the Photographic and Imaging
Department, British Museum and are copyright the Trustees
of the British Museum.

bpk/Ägyptisches Museum und Papyrussammlung, Staatliche
Museen zu Berlin. Photo: Margarete Büsing: 11 bottom
right; 12 top left.

bpk/Ägyptisches Museum und Papyrussammlung, Staatliche
Museen zu Berlin. Photo: Jürgen Liepe: 53 right; 67 top.

Egypt Exploration Society: 53 left.

Graham Harrison: 13 bottom left; 47 bottom right.

George Hart: 40 bottom right.

Angela McDonald: 11 top right; 12 bottom left; 13 bottom
centre; 13 bottom right; 18 bottom right; 25 bottom left; 26
bottom left; 26 bottom right; 28 left; 40 centre right; 42 top
left and bottom right; 44 top right; 45 top right; 45 bottom
right; 46 bottom left; 52 top left and bottom right; 54
bottom; 63 bottom; 66 bottom right; 69 top right.

© Geoffrey T. Martin: 52 top right.

© Photo RMN/© Hervé Levandowski: 49 top right.

A. Sorrell: Semna reconstruction on page 22.

Claire Thorne: maps on page 6 and 65.

Contents

Introduction

May the god put affection for me in people's hearts so that everyone will like me. May he give me a worthy burial in the cemetery of my city, for the Afterlife is under his command. May he make my name last like the stars in the sky while my statue remains one of his followers. May my soul be remembered in his temple night and day. May I relive my youth like the moon. May my name never, ever be forgotten in all the years to come.

Inscription of Montuemhat, Late Period.

Figure of an official cradling his soul (ba).

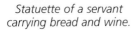

Statuette of a servant carrying bread and wine.

Who were the Egyptians? What were their lives like?

More than anything, the Egyptians wanted people to ask these questions. People who could afford it tried to leave some trace of themselves behind so that, long after their deaths, people would still say their names and talk about their deeds. Kings carved their victories on temple walls, and officials and priests commissioned statues that they hoped would stand for ever.

Noblemen designed their tombs to welcome visitors, putting bright images of their lives and beliefs on the walls and carving inscriptions by the entrance to encourage passers-by to pay attention to them.

The Egyptians did not put as much effort into temporary things. All villages and houses in Egypt were built of mud-brick. Over time they have been taken apart, or crumbled back into the earth. Very few survive, so when we want to ask questions about how the Egyptians lived, mostly we have to turn to their tombs and temples, and whatever was left in them. We can learn a lot from what the Egyptians left behind if we know how to read the evidence.

The aim of this book is to guide you through life in ancient Egypt and to explore what different jobs were like for the Egyptians of the past. Each chapter deals with one of the many different types of people, from kings to commoners, who made up ancient Egyptian society. Life was very different for a pharaoh and a farmer. Chapter by chapter, you will read about the lives, hopes and fears of the Egyptians in their own words, and you will see the art, objects and monuments which we use now to imagine what their world was like.

Model of a boat from a nobleman's tomb.

You will find maps of the places mentioned in the book and an Egyptian time-line on pages 6-7. If you would like to do some more exploring yourself, you can find suggestions for further reading on pages 78-79.

In the words of a Keeper of the King's Horses named Bakaa who lived in the time of Ramses II:

Delight! Have fun! This isn't a task that will weigh heavy on your hearts!

Cup in the shape of a lotus-flower designed to make the drinker feel young again.

Servants bringing offerings to their master's tomb.

The Delta

MEDITERRANEAN SEA

Alexandria •
• Avaris

Lower Egypt

Giza • • Tura
Saqqara • • Memphis

Dishasha •

EGYPT

• Bersha
• Amarna
• Hatnub

Asyut •

Upper Egypt

• Akhmim

RED SEA

Abydos •
Valley of the Kings •
Deir el-Medina • • Thebes
Gebelein •
• el-Kab
Edfu •

First cataract — Elephantine
Aswan
Beit el Wali •

Abu Simbel •
Buhen •

NUBIA

Semna • Second
cataract

Third
cataract • Tumbus

Fourth
cataract

Fifth
cataract

Map of Ancient Egypt

Egypt is divided into two parts by the shape of the Nile as it runs from the south to the Mediterranean in the north. These parts are known as the Delta and the Nile Valley.

Since the Nile was so important, the Egyptians let it guide their sense of direction. It flows from the south, so the southern part of Egypt was called 'Upper Egypt', and the northern 'Lower Egypt'! The Egyptians thought of their country in these two parts, and a common name for Egypt was 'The Two Lands'.

Every place in Egypt and Nubia mentioned in this book is marked on this map. Foreign places are shown on the map on page 65.

Time in Ancient Egypt

The ancient Egyptians measured time by the reigns of kings. Whenever a new king came to the throne the calendar was re-set to Year 1. It is now most convenient for us to talk about dynasties (or families) of kings rather than mentioning fixed dates. Dynasties are arranged into longer periods of time, now called 'Kingdoms'.

Every time kingship broke down and there was more than one person ruling Egypt at the same time – and that happened three times! – we call it an Intermediate Period. You can see how the thirty-one known dynasties fit into these periods in the Time-Line opposite.

Time-Line of Egyptian History

Predynastic Period – People live in scattered groups without a king.

Early Dynastic Period – Egypt is united under one king for the first time.

The Old Kingdom – Pyramids and Power
2686–2181 BC, Dynasties 3, 4, 5, 6

One block from the pyramid of Khufu or Khafre (Dynasty 4) at Giza could weigh up to one ton!

First Intermediate Period – Egypt is divided into provinces, each ruled by a different governor.

The Middle Kingdom – The Age of Story-Telling
2055–1650 BC, Dynasties 11, 12, 13, 14

For the first time, stories are written down. Some even poke fun at the king and the gods.

Second Intermediate Period – Egypt is divided again, and a dynasty of Asiatic kings known as the Hyksos rules in the Delta.

The New Kingdom – The Rise and Fall of the Egyptian Empire
1550–1069 BC
Dynasties 18, 19, 20

Amenhotep III (Dynasty 18) revelled in Egypt's wealth, building temples and palaces and hundreds of statues.

Third Intermediate Period – Power is divided between Libyan generals in the north and the priests of Amun in the south.

The Late Period – Nostalgia for the Glory Days
747–332 BC, Dynasties 25, 26, 27, 28, 29, 30, 31

This sphinx statue of Taharqa (Dynasty 25) is based on a Middle Kingdom model. He wears the twin cobras of Nubian kings.

The Greco-Roman Period – Ptolemies and Emperors
332 BC–395 AD

Alexander the Great loved Egypt and built a new capital city, Alexandria. Some of his statues look Greek, and some look entirely Egyptian.

The Byzantine Period – The end of ancient Egyptian religion.

The Islamic Period – Begins 639-42 AD with the Arab conquest of Egypt.

1 Kings and Queens

> How mighty is the Lord of his Realm –
> he's one in a million, when a
> thousand others are ordinary!
> How mighty is the Lord of his Realm –
> he's a breezy place that lets
> everyone sleep until dawn!
> How mighty is the Lord of his Realm –
> he's a mountain that shuts out
> tempests when the sky is stormy!
>
> From a Hymn to King Senwosret III, 12th Dynasty.

Every Egyptian king was expected to live up to an ideal – he had to look after his people, protect his country and expand its borders, and build temples to worship the gods. Through their successes in war and glories in building, kings hoped that their names would be, in the words of Queen Hatshepsut, 'eternal like the undying stars'. Kings walked like gods among their people, but their lives were often filled with challenges and danger. In this chapter we explore the duties and burdens faced by the king and his family, and find out what it meant to be royal in ancient Egypt.

The gloomy pharaoh. Senwosret III looks unhappy and troubled in all his statues. Did he want his people to know how hard it was to be a king?

The King, his Friends and his Foes

Egypt was surrounded by powerful enemies - the many city-states to the north-east in Palestine, Syria and Anatolia, the tribes of Libya to the west, and especially the chieftains of Nubia to the south (see maps on page 6 and page 65). By the New Kingdom, Egypt controlled much of their territory, but every newly-crowned king faced the danger of rebellion. Did this make them afraid? One of Egypt's mightiest pharaohs, Seti I, was in exactly this position after his father died. The Shosu tribes of Syria immediately started to make trouble in an attempt to break away from Egyptian control. Seti had the situation recorded on the walls of Karnak temple in Thebes where we can still read about it today:

His Majesty was told: 'The Syrians are planning a rebellion. Their chiefs are banded together and have made a stand on the hills of Palestine. They have stirred up trouble and panic with each one killing his neighbour. They completely ignore the laws of the Palace.' His Majesty was delighted by it! For this perfect god rejoiced at the beginning of battle, he revelled at entering it. His heart was thrilled by the sight of blood as he chopped off the rebels' heads. For it was the moment of trampling enemies that he loved more than the day of celebration. So his Majesty felled them all with one stroke! He has left them no heirs – any who do escape his hand are taken back to Egypt as captives.

King Ramses II, son of Seti I, is shown twice the size of his men to show how important he is.

Huge granite fist of a colossal statue of Ramses II from Memphis. It measures 1.3m across – about six times the width of this page!

Not every country was at war with Egypt. Many letters from the king's allies in the north have survived from the New Kingdom. They are written on clay tablets in cuneiform (a wedge-shaped script used outside Egypt as a universal diplomatic language). They must have been translated for the king when they arrived in Egypt. They are usually full of good wishes and address the king as 'my brother'. But foreign kings were quick to take offence. For example, King Burnaburiash of Babylonia is peeved that King Amenhotep IV has not sent him 'Get-well' wishes, even though he is told that Egypt is a long way away. Burnaburiash writes:

For my brother – a mighty king – is there really a land that is far distant and one that is close by?

Even when diplomatic relations between Egypt and its northern allies were at their friendliest (at least on the surface!), the king of Egypt continued to have himself shown striking ('smiting') his enemies. Smiting scenes date back to the beginning of Egyptian history and continue until its end.

Ivory tag showing the 1st Dynasty King Den smiting an enemy. The tag was actually a label for his sandals.

Kings at Rest and Play

Official inscriptions tell us little about how kings relaxed. For that we have to turn to stories, which sometimes paint a rather cheeky picture. One papyrus, known as 'The Tales of Wonder', describes how King Snofru calls on the magician Djadjaemankh because he is bored and cannot find anything to do by himself. He is happy to take up the magician's suggestion that he assemble a crew of pretty girls to row him around the palace lake. But as soon as there is a problem (one of the ladies drops her pendant in the water and refuses to row), the king is helpless again.

Not all kings needed help to amuse themselves. Horsemanship was considered a kingly skill, and so was archery. The hunting of dangerous animals like lions and wild bulls was also a royal sport and kings

Cuneiform letter from King Tushratta of Mitanni in Syria. He wishes King Amenhotep III a speedy recovery and tells him that he is sending along a statue of the goddess of healing, Ishtar, to help him feel better. The writing in ink is Egyptian and records when the letter arrived.

are often shown pitting themselves against these creatures - almost always single-handedly.

King Amenhotep III wanted everyone to know about his hunting skills. He had notices carved on the back of scarab-beetle ornaments that he gave out to his officials and friends. One tells us that he personally killed 94 bulls in less than a week. The one shown below is about lion-hunting:

Total number of lions which His Majesty has brought down with his own arrows from year 1 to year 10: 102 fierce lions!

King Ramses III hunting wild bulls, Medinet Habu temple, Thebes.

The Royal Family

A good wife could be a great advantage to a king. Some queens seem to have been almost as powerful as their husbands. Queen Tiye, the wife of Amenhotep III, wrote to Egypt's allies after her husband's death, before power was transferred to her son. Her statues show her as a strong-willed woman with intense eyes and a determined set to her mouth.

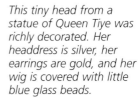

This tiny head from a statue of Queen Tiye was richly decorated. Her headdress is silver, her earrings are gold, and her wig is covered with little blue glass beads.

Akhenaten and Nefertiti hugging their children.

The sweetest representations of family life come from the troubled reign of Tiye's son, Amenhotep IV, who renamed himself Akhenaten and quickly turned Egypt upside down. His love for his wife, Nefertiti, and their six daughters is obvious in all their family portraits. Akhenaten made his people worship his family alongside his new god, the Aten, instead of traditional gods like Amun and Osiris. This made his people very unhappy. As soon as Akhenaten died, his city and his new style of life were abandoned, and images of his family were attacked.

Ramses' temple   Nefertari's temple

Queens as Kings

For the Egyptians, there was no such thing as a female monarch. Their word for 'queen' simply means 'king's wife'. However, we know of many very powerful royal women. Some were given special honours by their royal husbands and sons. Queen Ahmose-Nefertari (right) was named High Priestess of Amun when she was alive, and was treated as a goddess after she died. People were still praying to her 400 years later.

Queens sometimes took over if their husbands died suddenly, or if their sons were too young to rule alone. Most queens quietly supported the king behind the scenes. But some queens stand out.

At Abu Simbel (left), Ramses II showed his love for his beautiful queen Nefertari by building her a temple alongside his.

We know of a Queen Sobeknefru who ruled in the 12th Dynasty and took royal names like a king. This seal (left) shows her name. The most notorious queen was Hatshepsut. After her husband, King Thutmosis II, died she stepped forward to help his very young son, Thutmosis III. After a few years, however, she declared herself 'king'. She commanded the army, sent trading missions abroad and built many fine monuments. After about 20 years, Hatshepsut disappeared, leaving the grown-up Thutmosis III to rule alone. He became one of Egypt's mightiest warrior-pharaohs. Late in his reign, he attacked Hatshepsut's monuments. He even bricked up her obelisks at Karnak temple in Thebes. But the bricks protected the obelisks, so we can still read Hatshepsut's words carved in clear hieroglyphs:

What will people say, those who shall
see my monuments in later times?

Did she ever dream that we would still be talking about her thousands of years later?

Hatshepsut even had herself shown as a male king in temple carvings.

Hatshepsut's name, carved in hieroglyphs on her obelisk at Karnak.

A Ghostly King

It seems that even a strong king could find himself in danger. The first king of the Middle Kingdom, Amenemhat I, suffered the worst fate that could befall a ruler: he was murdered by his own guards. In a story that was written after his death, the king's ghost gives gloomy warnings to his son:

Beware of subjects who are nobodies for you're not aware of their plotting. Don't trust a brother, don't confide in a friend, don't take any confidants – it will do no good. When you lie down, guard your heart yourself, for no one has helpers on the day of trouble ...

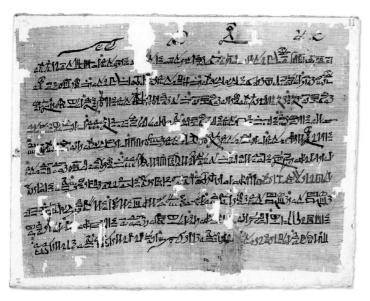

Papyrus with a copy of King Amenemhat I's story.

Royal Names and Regalia

Crowns and headdresses
You can always recognize a king by the royal cobra ('uraeus') on his brow. According to myth, it could spit fire at the king's enemies. Queens sometimes wear a uraeus too (left).

Kings also wore a crown. There are many Egyptian crowns. The two most important are the White Crown of the south and the Red Crown of the north. Often kings wore both together as the Double Crown (left) to show they ruled all of Egypt.

The striped cloth *nemes* headdress (below) was also very common. This example is being worn by a small figure of King Seti I.

The Double Crown (above) and the nemes headdress (right).

The king's five names
Kings took five royal names, but they mostly used just two, the 'birth name' and the 'throne name'. Both were written in oval rings called cartouches (you can see them beside Ramses III, left).

The 'Two Ladies' name put the king under the protection of the goddesses of the north and south, Wadjet and Nekhbet.

The earliest kings were known only by their 'Horus name' which linked the king with the falcon-god. The Horus name was written inside a rectangular box called a *serekh* with a falcon perched on top (right).

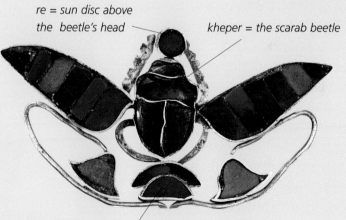

re = sun disc above the beetle's head

kheper = the scarab beetle

Kha = the rising sun beneath the beetle's body

Names in hieroglyphs could be 'hidden' in the king's jewellery or regalia. This amulet 'spells out' Khakheperre, the throne name of King Senwosret II.

Noblemen wore jewellery and fine clothes, but only kings (and gods) wore a bull's tail around their waist. Ramses III (above) also carries the crook and flail of the first god-king, Osiris, and wears the White Crown.

2 Officials and Scribes

Nurture writings in your heart and, see! You'll be sheltered from every kind of toil. You can become an important official. Remember, will you, what happens to the man who has no skill? No one even knows his name! He is loaded down before the eyes of the scribe who knows himself.

Papyrus Lansing, New Kingdom.

We can roughly divide Egypt's population into two parts – those who performed physical tasks like building or farming and the officials who oversaw them. Many Egyptian texts, like the papyrus above, are extremely frank in their descriptions of how miserable it was to be anything other than an official. In practice, a great burden of responsibility sat squarely on the shoulders of Egypt's administrators, and their jobs were often hard. In this chapter, we explore the duties that officials performed for their king and country.

The Highest Officials – The Vizier

The highest official, second only to the king, was the vizier (*tjaty* in Egyptian), who acted as a kind of prime minister. The vizier was very often a relative of the king. He supervised the governors of all the provinces of Egypt. By the 18th Dynasty, there was a northern vizier based at Memphis and also a southern vizier based at Thebes.

The vizier in his official robes.

Painted wooden statue of an official whose name has been lost. His authority is symbolized by the long staff he holds.

The Insignia of Office

Egyptian art had different ways of showing high status among officials. You can find status symbols everywhere.

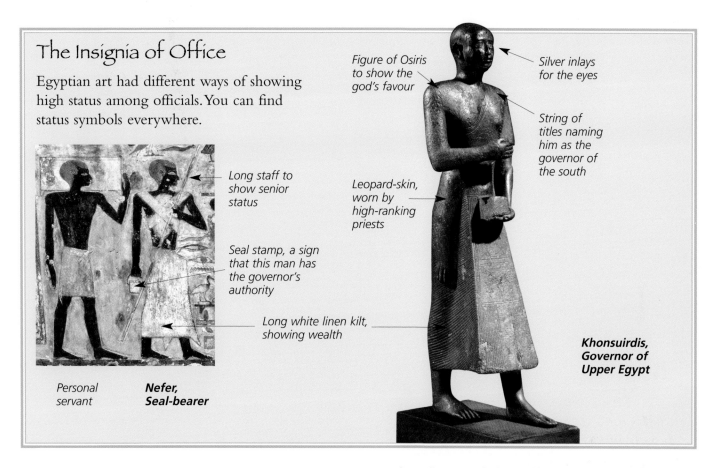

Figure of Osiris to show the god's favour

Silver inlays for the eyes

String of titles naming him as the governor of the south

Long staff to show senior status

Leopard-skin, worn by high-ranking priests

Seal stamp, a sign that this man has the governor's authority

Long white linen kilt, showing wealth

Personal servant

Nefer, Seal-bearer

Khonsuirdis, Governor of Upper Egypt

In the New Kingdom, a text called 'The Duties of the Vizier' gives us an idea of the vizier's many responsibilities. It tells us that he judged disputes, passed sentences on criminals, gave the army their orders and sent men and women to do all sorts of duties, from farming to quarrying stone for royal buildings.

The vizier's office was the nerve-centre for the kingdom. He is described almost like a king at his daily meetings with his staff:

As for all acts of this official, the Vizier, when he holds an audience within the Vizier's Hall – he shall sit upon an official chair, with a red carpet upon the ground, wearing his official cloak, with one animal pelt supporting his back and another under his feet, while his staff of office is in his hand. The forty leather rolls shall be opened in his presence, while the southern chiefs wait in the two aisles in front of him, the chief steward at his right, the chief security officer on his left, and the Vizier's scribes by his side.

The Royal Treasurer

Every day the vizier and the royal treasurer made reports to one another. Their words are recorded:

ROYAL TREASURER: 'All your concerns are safe and sound; all the officials responsible for them have reported to me, saying: "All your concerns are safe and sound." And so, the Palace is safe and sound.'

VIZIER: 'All your concerns are safe and sound. Every part of the Residence is safe and sound. The closing of the sealed chambers to date and their opening to date has been reported to me by the officials responsible for them.'

The royal treasurer takes responsibility for the palace, while the vizier reports on the 'Residence' – the capital city as a whole. The royal treasury must have been filled with riches gathered in taxes at home and abroad. There was a steady flow of precious goods into Egypt from the lands the king conquered in battle: gold, silver, fine clothes, animal pelts, weapons, and even food and wine.

Nubians bringing precious goods into Egypt for the king, painted in the tomb of Sobekhotep.

The Chief Architect

The next most important official in Egypt bore the title 'Overseer of All the King's Works'. He was the chief architect in charge of the king's building projects – from the pyramids of the Old Kingdom to the grand temples of the New Kingdom. One man could be both vizier and chief architect and thus wield great power. One such man was Imhotep (right), who worked for King Djoser of the 3rd Dynasty. Imhotep invented the first pyramid of Egypt, the Step Pyramid complex at Saqqara (below). This was the first monumental building to be made entirely of stone. Imhotep's wisdom and learning was famous and eventually he was worshipped as a god of healing. Archaeologists are still searching the sands of Saqqara for his tomb.

The Step Pyramid of King Djoser at Saqqara.

The Greatest of the Great – The Case of Senenmut

One particular official was determined to become famous. His name was Senenmut and he lived in the time of Queen Hatshepsut. He gained immense power even though he came from a humble family. He began his career as a minor official, perhaps a soldier, but the queen made him special tutor to her daughter, Neferura. Senenmut had several statues made showing himself embracing the young princess (left).

When Hatshepsut declared herself 'king', Senenmut was involved in almost all areas of royal life. His titles tell us that he was responsible for the estates belonging to the god Amun's temple at Karnak in Thebes, that he oversaw the royal treasury and that he acted as chief architect as well. In his inscription on a statue from Karnak, he boasts:

> I acted as the Chief of Chiefs,
> the Overseer of Overseers of All Works ...
> I was the Greatest of the Great in the whole land!

Senenmut began work on two tombs, one right beside Hatshepsut's temple at Thebes. Within the temple itself, he had secret images of himself carved in some of its doorways – something that no one else in Egypt had ever done.

We do not know when or how Senenmut died, but he was not buried in either of his tombs. At some point after his death, his name was attacked both in his tombs and on his statues, just like Hatshepsut's. Who did it? We might never know. Senenmut himself certainly did not predict his fall from grace. On one of his statues, he confidently states:

> My good name will persist with people
> throughout the years to come!

In this statue the princess Neferura is wrapped up in Senenmut's cloak. This is unusual. Does it suggest that he is protecting her, almost like a father?

Administrators

The Egyptian system of administration relied upon many provincial governors who reported to the vizier. The efficiency and the loyalty of these men must have depended very much upon the authority of both the king and the vizier. Provincial governors reported to the vizier, but it was up to the king to assign them their duties in particular areas and to keep an eye on their activities. In those periods when they were allowed too much freedom – for example at the end of the Old Kingdom – trouble always followed for the king. Local governors could become extremely corrupt.

One Old Kingdom letter from Aswan survives complaining about the local governor, Sabni. It accuses Sabni of robbing a fellow official. However, it is likely that he never faced punishment, since he was buried in a spacious, lavishly decorated tomb in the cliffs overlooking the town.

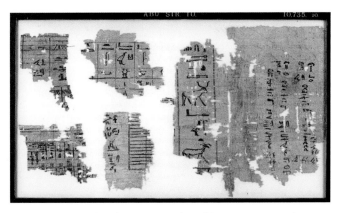

Egyptian administrators produced huge amounts of paperwork. The Abusir papyri are the oldest surviving examples. They deal with the staff and equipment of the funerary temple of King Neferirkare of the 5th Dynasty.

A Scribe's Equipment

The most basic piece of equipment for a scribe was his palette. This was a rectangular case, usually made of wood, which had a slot for reed pens and often two inkwells (one for black, one for red). It was light and could be tucked under the arm (right).

Scribe painted on the wall of the tomb-chapel of Nebamun.

A scribe's palette, made of wood.

Official records were made on sheets of papyrus, but scraps of pottery (called *ostraca*) were used for notes. Documents on papyrus were rolled up and kept in special cases. The scribe Nebseni wanted to take his papyrus carrying-case with him into the Afterlife. It is tucked under his chair in this picture (left) from a papyrus placed in his tomb.

Scribes and Official Records

Most of the important work carried out by the king's administrators relied upon professional writers (scribes). Scribes were trained from a young age. They learned to read and write by copying texts that promised them high office, friendship with the king, free passage in treasuries and granaries, and great personal wealth. But these privileges were only offered to a tiny number of people. It is estimated now that only 1 per cent of Egypt's population could read and write.

Those who did learn to read and write could work either for individuals or for the state, keeping records and carrying messages. If they did well, they could end up controlling the vast resources of a major temple, or even of the palace itself.

Writing was central to the running of the country, and officials of all levels must have relied upon scribes. Perhaps not every high official could read and write for himself, but this was certainly the impression that they wanted to give. From the Old Kingdom on, officials commissioned statues of themselves in the scribal pose (right) because of the prestige and wisdom that was associated with being able to read and write.

Scribes are shown making official records of many different kinds. Sometimes they count animals on an estate so they can tax the owner, and sometimes they count how many enemy hands were cut off after a battle!

Passhuper in the pose typical of scribes – cross-legged with a papyrus roll stretched over his knees. His ink blocks are by his left hand. His right hand is poised to grasp a reed brush for writing. He is shown as a young man, but his stomach is rippled with fat. This was how Egyptian artists showed that a person was rich enough to afford lots of food.

The Egyptians must have written thousands of documents, and only a small proportion of them have survived. We still get the strong impression that the Egyptians recorded every official activity very carefully.

In the Middle Kingdom, several fortresses were built in Nubia. Each fortress had its own commander and garrison of troops. We have a fragmentary set of papyrus documents from the fortress at Semna (below). These were written by a military scribe based at the fortress who sent them to a high official in Thebes. It is clear from these remarkable records that the soldiers at Semna were watching every movement of the local tribes. They sent their detailed reports to Thebes for approval and for orders.

Large flake of pottery (ostracon) recording workmen's absences from work with the dates and their excuses.

(Above) Drawing of the Fortress of Semna in Nubia, and (below) the Semna Despatches that were sent from it.

The Egyptians also kept records of people who worked for the state. Our best evidence comes from the village at Deir el-Medina. The workmen who built the tombs of the Valley of the Kings lived there with their families. Strictly speaking, the working week was ten days with one day of rest. In fact, the workmen had many more days off. Some were official holidays for religious festivals, but many more were for private reasons.

Workmen were allowed to take time off work, but scribes carefully recorded all their days off. The reasons for absence include personal illness, births, and deaths. The records are detailed, but were they true? Thousands of years later, we see workmen claiming that the same relative has died twice!

The Immortality of Writers

Apprentice scribes were promised the chance of immortality if they followed in the footsteps of famous writers of the past like Khakheperresoneb (below). It is likely that the famous literary works that survive today – such as 'The Tale of Sinuhe' – were commissioned by the king or a high official. We never learn the names of their authors. But 'Wisdom Texts' were different. These took the form of instructions passed on from a wise man (usually to his son) explaining how to live properly. Texts like this are always linked with specific men, like Imhotep, Ptahhotep and Ani. The names of these writers became legendary.

Being a scribe meant high status, no hard manual work, and the promise of immortality. This may help us understand the purpose of this little vessel in the shape of a rather chubby, and slightly wobbly, scribe (right). It seems to promise anyone who uses it prosperity and (tipsy!) happiness.

A vessel in the shape of an unbalanced (!) scribe. His position might suggest that the scribe is wealthy enough to get very drunk.

Wooden board with a copy of 'The Complaints of Khakheperresoneb'. It is a Wisdom Text described as 'A gathering of words, a heaping of sayings, a search for phrases by a curious heart'. It describes the terrible state of the world when people do not live properly.

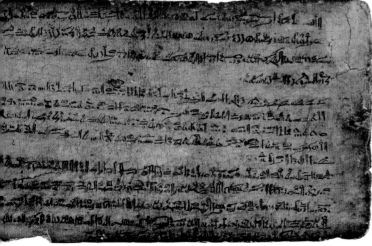

3 Priests and Priestesses

I am one who enters the world of the dead, who opens the burial chamber and who knows the secrets of the mysterious sanctuaries. I am the official who has access to the majesty of the king.

Inscription of Menkheperresoneb, the High Priest of Amun, 18th Dynasty.

The priests and priestesses of ancient Egypt performed two important duties. They looked after the gods in their temples and they provided food and drink for the dead. In return for their services, priests and priestesses were held in high esteem – the more exalted the god or person they cared for, the higher their own status was. In fact, as we shall see in this chapter, at certain points in history the privileges and power of priests and priestesses even rivalled that of the king.

The Duties of the Priesthood

Priests and priestesses had many duties. If they worked in a temple, they looked after the statue of the god or king that lived inside the sanctuary. To the Egyptians, this statue was alive. Three or four times a day, priests brought food and drink to the statue to let it feed on the aromas. They also burned incense to soothe it. Priestesses, often from royal or noble families, provided entertainment, music and dancing. The same was done for the statues of important noblemen in their tombs.

Hieroglyph for 'pure' or 'pure-priest'.

A priest performing duties for the dead, burning incense and pouring water. His leopard-skin cloak tells us he is a sem-priest (see page 26).

Copper pendant showing a priest kneeling by an offering table. The frog is a symbol of renewed life. The little priest figure symbolizes an eternity of service – carved in front of him are two round loaves of bread and two vessels for beer or water.

In large temples like Karnak in Thebes, priests also oversaw the craftsmen who produced items for a god's use and the labourers who worked the temple's lands and looked after its animals. But before the New Kingdom, this was mostly done by part-time priests who worked in teams called 'phyles' for only a few months each year. For the rest of the year, many of these part-time priests went home to farm their land.

On duty, all priests and priestesses had to be 'pure'. The Greek historian Herodotus tells us that the priests he met on his travels in Egypt were only supposed to wear handmade linen garments and papyrus sandals. They also shaved off all the hair from their bodies. In earlier times, some priests did shave their heads, but they made themselves pure mainly by washing. The high priest Anhurmose describes himself as:

a pure man with covered hands and washed fingers who pleased the gods.

High Priests

Only the highest orders of priests could actually touch a god's statue. They washed, anointed, and even clothed the statue each day. In theory, the king himself was supposed to perform the daily rituals for each deity in Egypt. But he could not be everywhere at once, so high priests acted as his deputies. This gave high priests powers dangerously close to those of the king himself. The High Priest of Amun at Karnak during the New Kingdom was undoubtedly the most powerful priest in Egypt. He controlled the temple's vast resources, including its hundreds of staff. Many High Priests of Amun were very ambitious men. A good example is Menkheperresoneb. He is known as both a Second Priest of Amun (the High Priest's deputy)

Statue of Menkheperresoneb, the High Priest of Amun in Karnak temple (shown left). The statue was made when he was still deputy High Priest.

and then as High Priest himself under King Thutmosis III. Early in his career he began work on a tomb on the West Bank of Thebes, but when he became High Priest, he started a second one in a more prestigious position high up in the cliffs. He ended up being buried in his original tomb, because he ran out of time or money to finish his second! The walls of this later tomb show his many duties for the temple. He received rich tribute from foreign nations to the north and south, and oversaw the temple craftsmen who manufactured ritual and military items. One of the many titles he lists for himself may explain his rise to power: 'The Priest whom the Sovereign Loves'.

High Priests like Menkheperresoneb depended on the king to promote them, but by the end of the New Kingdom the high priests were powerful enough in their own right to challenge the king's authority. Some were very bold and went as far as writing their names in royal cartouches, like kings.

Types of Priest

The most important priests were called *hemu-netjer*, which means 'servants of god'. The High Priest was called the 'First *Hem-Netjer*'. *Wab*-priests (*wab* means 'pure') were of a slightly lower rank. In addition to these two categories of priest who managed the daily running of a temple there were also those whose duties were more specialized. 'Hour-priests' were astronomers and made sure that rituals were carried out at their correct times. '*Sem*-priests' (sometimes called '*Setem*-priests') performed the important 'Opening of the Mouth' ceremony which had the power to bring either a statue or a mummy to life again. You can recognize them by the special leopard-skin cloaks they wore (as in the main picture on page 24).

Lector-priests could read and write and so were responsible for a temple's library of ritual papyri: their Egyptian title means 'Carriers of the Sacred Scrolls'. Like the priests of the lioness-goddess

Scenes from Karnak temple, Thebes.

(Left) The High Priest Amenhotep holding a bouquet before King Ramses XI. In the morning sun, the king disappears into shadow!

(Right) The High Priest Amenhotep being rewarded by King Ramses XI. He is shown as tall as the king, which is very unusual.

Kah offers to Osiris, the Goddess of the West, and Anubis. Priests poured offerings of wine, beer, milk and water for the gods and also for the dead.

Head of a statue of a 'Bald One of Hathor'.

Another group of priests were known as 'The Bald Ones of Hathor'. Their distinctive statues show them sitting with a Hathor shrine cradled on their knees. They usually have one hand cupped to their mouth, ready to receive offerings of beer. The statues are usually described as 'guardians' and they seem to have been positioned at the entrance to sanctuaries of Hathor and other goddesses. Appeals to visitors are carved onto the statues' bodies – they promise that all prayers will be passed on to the goddess of the sanctuary in return for food and especially drink offerings. This was carved on the statue of Ameneminet:

Pour beer into my hand and date juice into my mouth; put fragrant oil on my bald head and a garland of fresh flowers around my neck; make an offering for me with wine and beer, because I'm a Bald One of the Golden Goddess. If there's no beer, give me some fresh water because, certainly, the Mistress likes her Bald One to be happy!

Sekhmet (left), they were considered to have healing power and acted as doctors. In literary tales, they often appear as skilled magicians because of their access to their temple's secrets. The Middle Kingdom story known as 'The Tales of Wonder' describes the miracles performed by powerful magician lector-priests. Djadjaemankh parts the waters of a lake just so that a rowing girl can find the pendant she has dropped. Djedi is able to re-attach the severed head of a goose before King Khufu's very eyes.

Statues of Sekhmet were made to ward off illness and misfortune. King Amenhotep III had hundreds of them made.

Statue of Peraha showing him cupping a hand to his mouth, like a Bald One.

The Tools of Ritual

(left) King Seti I offers incense to the gods in his temple at Abydos. He holds an incense burner with a falcon's head at one end and a human hand at the other. The bowl containing the burning incense rests in this hand. You can see the same features on the real incense burner shown below. It includes a tiny figure of a priest kneeling beside a cartouche-shaped bowl. The falcon and the cartouche are both symbols of the king.

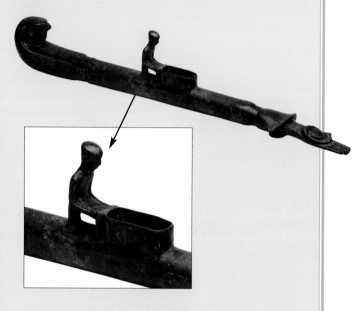

Bronze tongs like the ones shown on the left were used to handle balls of incense. They are shaped like human hands. These tongs come from the city of Amarna.

Women in the Priesthood

Until the late New Kingdom, women only took part in a few priestly activities. High-status women often held the title of 'Songstress', linking them with temple entertainment. In the Old Kingdom, women who held the title 'priestess' mostly served female deities such as Hathor. One exception is the cult of the fertility god Min at Akhmim, which had priestesses called 'Watchers of Min'. We don't know their exact duties. One woman named Henet who held the title in the 6th Dynasty was also a priestess of Hathor and, more unusually, an 'Overseer of the Musicians' which meant she had authority over both men and women.

Ankhnesneferibre, a God's Wife of Amun, had this beautifully-carved lid made for her sarcophagus (stone coffin).

One of the most important priestesses was known as the 'God's Wife of Amun'. In the New Kingdom this priestess was usually a queen. It was a powerful position, and Queen Hatshepsut used it to help her become 'king'.

This noblewoman's name is unknown, but she carries a sistrum-rattle. Temple musicians played these instruments for gods and goddesses.

The God's Wives of the 25th Dynasty had their own tombs and chapels inside Medinet Habu temple at Thebes. At that time, the God's Wives were forbidden to marry and so they had to adopt their successors. In this way, their authority was strictly controlled. We sometimes know little about these important women except their names, but the strength of their characters shines through in their proud portraits.

4 Households and Families

If you're brave and can control your feelings, you'll fill your arms with your children, you'll kiss your wife, and you'll see your home!

'The Tale of the Shipwrecked Sailor', Middle Kingdom.

One of the Egyptian words for 'family' was pronounced *abet* – it meant 'the thing you wish for'. Having a family was vital to the Egyptians, because it guaranteed the survival of their households, the official posts they held, their position in society, and – most important of all – their names. In his tomb at Thebes, the nobleman Amenemhat makes this wish for all those who will make offerings for him:

May your name endure on the lips of your children for ever!

There is plenty of evidence to tell us that it was not always easy to set up a household and bring up a family. In this chapter, we find out what having a family meant to the Egyptians – its challenges, joys and sorrows.

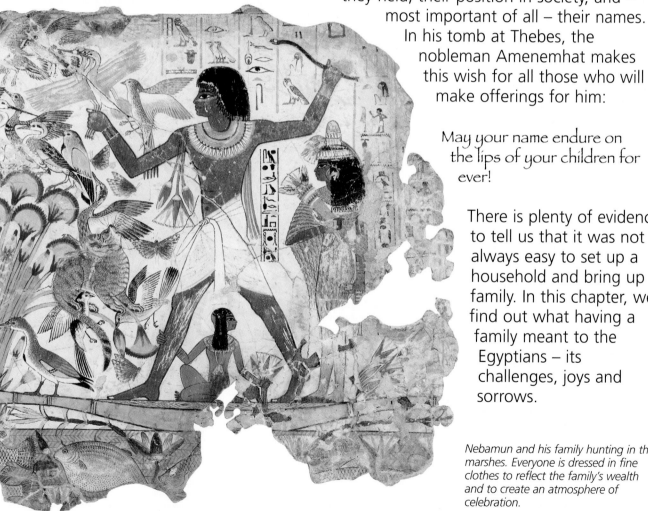

Nebamun and his family hunting in the marshes. Everyone is dressed in fine clothes to reflect the family's wealth and to create an atmosphere of celebration.

The Family Home

A typical Egyptian household was made up of a man and woman, their children, and possibly some members of the extended family, like brothers and sisters or parents. If it was a wealthy household, there could also be a number of servants living with the family who would manage daily chores as well as a nurse to tend to young children.

Modern Egyptian towns have often been built on top of ancient ones, so there are only a few places, like Amarna and Deir el-Medina, where ancient Egyptian houses survive. In a typical house, the front door opened on to a room used by the women of the household. We know this because the walls are usually decorated with images of Bes and Taweret, gods who looked after women and children. A door at the back of this first room led to a more private living area. This held a stone altar where the family could pray to the gods and honour their ancestors. Kitchens and storerooms for food and equipment were at the back of the house. The servants probably spent most of their time there.

Larger houses had other smaller rooms leading off the main living room, which might have been working areas or private bedrooms. The grandest houses had up to seventy rooms.

Houses had one or more storeys. In modern Egyptian villages, people use the flat rooftops for working and playing during the day, and for sleeping at night. Ancient Egyptian families probably did the same.

Model houses like these two come from tombs. They are our best evidence of what real houses looked like.

Some larger houses had shady private gardens with tree-lined ponds, like this one (above) painted in the tomb-chapel of Nebamun. The Egyptians enjoyed beauty. One New Kingdom papyrus says:

Create a garden in addition to the land that you work ... fill your hand with flowers that your eye can feast on.

Husbands and Wives

Statue of Katep and his wife Hetepheres. Hetepheres is paler than her husband because rich women would spend most of their time indoors, sheltered from the sun.

Men whose wives had died often re-married. A letter from the Middle Kingdom tells us that sometimes new wives found it difficult to fit into their husband's home. It was written by a man named Hekanakht (see page 39) and was brought to his family by his secretary Sahathor. Hekanakht sternly warns his sons to be kind to his new wife:

> Now throw that maid Senen out of my house - see here! - whenever Sahathor reaches you, because if she spends just one more day in my house, action will be taken! You are standing back and letting her mistreat my new wife.

Stela (carved stone) of Kawer Intef who is shown with all three of his wives standing behind him.

For most of ancient Egyptian history there was no formal wedding ceremony. The Egyptian word for 'marriage' simply means 'setting up a household'.

Wealthy men could have as many wives as they liked. Kings had hundreds! In a household with many wives, there was one principal wife (like the Principal Queen in the palace) and she was shown beside her husband in statues and on tomb walls. That actually makes it difficult for us to tell if a man had more than one wife, although sometimes it is more obvious (like Kawer Intef's family, right).

Mothers and Children

Children were the main reason for setting up a household. If a woman could not give her husband children, he would probably divorce her. Some divorced women went back to their parents' households, but many ended up as servants. Within the home, women did jobs like brewing and weaving, but they relied on their husbands to support them.

For this reason, women prayed to goddesses like Hathor and Isis to grant them a child. They also relied heavily on magic during their pregnancy and especially as they were about to give birth.

In the ancient world, many women died in childbirth. Only magical objects showed pictures of pregnant women because it was such a dangerous condition in those days. Most of the time, when pregnant women are shown, their stomachs are only slightly rounded (below).

Magical jug in the shape of a pregnant woman, maybe used by a woman who wanted to have a baby.

A painted ostracon (flake of pottery) from the village of Deir el-Medina shows a new mother sitting in a leafy pavilion with her maid (above, right). This suggests that childbirth happened outside the house – possibly in pavilions set up on the roofs of houses. After children were born, parents prayed to deities like Taweret and Bes to protect them. These gods look frightening, but they were kind protectors.

Hieroglyph showing a woman giving birth – but her stomach is only slightly rounded.

Taweret has the form of a fierce hippopotamus with sharp teeth and a crocodile tail. Bes is shown as a dwarf with a lion's face. Both of them protected mothers and children.

Magic for Children

If babies or young children fell ill, there was usually very little Egyptian medicine could do. But there were lots of magical spells to protect children. Some of these spells sound extremely sinister because they describe illnesses as the work of evil demons. One spell addresses demons who come in the night to do harm:

Have you come to kiss this child? I will not let you kiss him!
Have you come to bring silence? I will not allow the causing of silence in him!
Have you come to hurt him? I will not let you hurt him!
Have you come to take him?
I will not let you take him from me!

Coffin of a young child whose bones show signs of a serious illness.

Children and parents wore amulets to protect them from harm. One of the most common was in the shape of an eye.

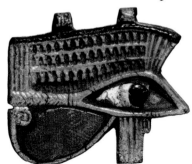

An eye-shaped amulet called wedjat (meaning 'safety') in Egyptian.

One special amulet was made only for children. It was a piece of papyrus, rolled up and placed inside a tube that the child wore like a necklace. The papyrus recorded an agreement made by the child's parents with several gods. In return for offerings, these gods promised to keep the child safe. This is from an amulet made for a girl called Buiruharkhons:

We will protect her from collapsing walls and from thunderbolts ...
We will protect her from every death, from every illness, from every accusation, from every wrong, from every confusion, from every frustration, from every unpleasant word, from every nasty word, from every cruel word, and from every kind of teasing ...
We will protect her from heart-break and heart-ache ...
We will protect her on a ship, on the desert-edge, and on any kind of journey which she might make to any place she wants.
We will provide everything that is good for her, every useful piece of magic, and a happy childhood.

Parents faced other problems. One craftsman was left with three daughters after his wife died. He had to leave his village for several days at a time to work, so it was not easy for him to look after them. But he swore an oath in front of his whole village never to be separated from his children.

Children in Art

Children are usually naked in Egyptian art to show their youth. They are often shown much smaller than adults. Iry's son (right) hardly comes up to his father's knees.

Both boys and girls have shaved heads but wear one long ponytail of hair which is known as the 'sidelock of youth'. Inherkhau's son (below, right) also has two strands falling onto his forehead in a kind of fringe. This style became common in the New Kingdom.

Adults and children both used black kohl to frame their eyes. This was not just to look good – the kohl protected their eyes from infections as well.

Both adults and children wore jewellery as a sign of wealth. Nebamun's daughter (below) has gold earrings, many gold bangles, and a colourful collar around her neck and shoulders with a lotus flower pendant. Inherkhau's son has a collar just like his father's and wears silver earrings. Curiously, adult men are very rarely shown wearing earrings.

The nobleman Iry's son, called 'Iry junior'.

Nebamun's daughter. We do not know her name.

The foreman Inherkhau and his son.

Children and Education

Egyptian children began their education at an early age. An official named Nefersekheru tells us:

I spent my youth of 10 years as a child upon the arm of my father, and I was taught to write.

Boys from rich families went to school and could become scribes like Nefersekheru. Most boys were trained in the profession of their father in the hope that they would inherit his position one day. Sensobek (shown on the stela below) became an overseer of priests like his father Intef. The two men look almost identical. They hold the same staff and sceptre and wear the same kind of kilt and collar. This is a clever way of showing that Sensobek has followed in his father's footsteps.

On the other hand, we know very little about the education of girls. Perhaps some girls learned to read and write, but if they did, this was only for fun. Girls could not become scribes or officials. Instead, they learned from their mothers how to spin, weave, brew and bake. If they were from wealthy families, they learned to supervise the work of servants.

For those who had worked hard for their position in society, it was important to hand that position to their children. Fathers saw this as their duty to their family, and in return they expected their children to support them in their old age (below).

Sensobek

Intef

577

A statue of a nobleman. Behind him, there is a tiny figure of his young son, supporting his father's leg and urging him on.

2319

Fun and Games

An assortment of children's toys from Egypt - the spinning tops and balls are from the Greco-Roman Period.

This little wooden cat was made in the New Kingdom. Pulling the string opens its mouth to reveal a set of sharp bronze teeth. It once had rock-crystal eyes and must have been a prized possession.

Two children's games are shown in this relief from an Old Kingdom tomb. One (right) is called a 'dance' and may be connected to a harvest ritual, because some of the children carry ears of grain in one hand and a knife for cutting them in the other.

This game (left) looks like a combination of hide-and-seek and wrestling. One boy has been caught inside his hiding place by three others. One of them holds him down. Another boy outside calls to him, 'You should escape from him – the one who's with you!'

5 Farmers and Herdsmen

The farmer wails more than the guinea fowl, his voice is louder than a raven's! His fingers are swollen – and so smelly!

'The Satire of the Trades', Middle Kingdom.

When the Egyptians imagined Paradise, they thought of broad fields with rich harvests, shady trees and overflowing streams – just like their life on earth, but without all the hardships.

Farmers and herdsmen provided food for people and for the worship of the gods. But they always worried - would it be a good year? They needed to produce enough to feed their families and animals and pay their taxes, as well as leaving extra to pay for next year's crop. Both farmers and herdsmen were at the mercy of the river Nile.

This chapter explores some of the trials and tribulations of the people who worked the land.

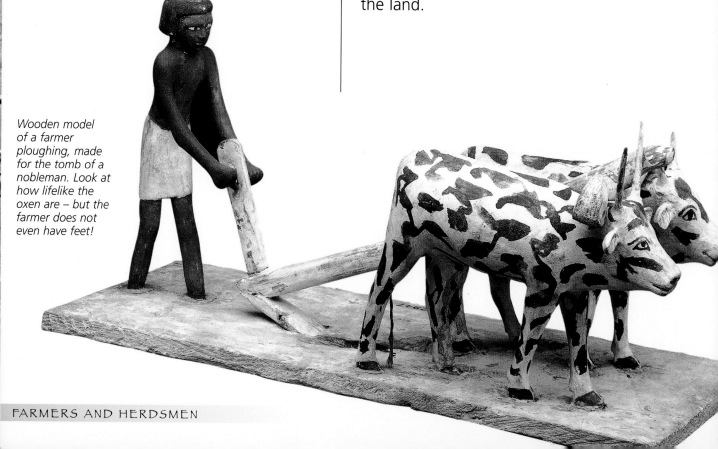

Wooden model of a farmer ploughing, made for the tomb of a nobleman. Look at how lifelike the oxen are – but the farmer does not even have feet!

A Farmer's Story

About four thousand years ago, a farmer named Hekanakht owned lands near Memphis. He grew barley and emmer to make bread and beer, and flax to make cloth. His brother Merisu managed the estate, because Hekanakht spent much of the year in the south looking after a nobleman's tomb. Hekanakht's secretary, Sahathor, carried letters back and forth for his master.

The servants of the nobleman Khaemwaset carry away freshly-cut crops from his fields.

From these letters, we learn that, at first, Hekanakht's estate was doing very well. His latest harvest had provided him with 510 sacks of grain. Grain was used as money in Egypt, so 65 sacks went to the state as taxes, and 130 sacks to his family as payment for their work on the estate. This left Hekanakht with plenty of grain to keep for a rainy day. Just over a year and a half later, Hekanakht's luck changed. His fields had not yielded a good harvest. He warned his family not to complain - at least they were eating, he said - but he himself was very unhappy about being sent old grain from the 'rainy-day' stock instead of fresh supplies. We have his sarcastic complaint to Merisu in his own handwriting:

Tomb model of a granary. A scribe is sitting on the roof, supervising. In the courtyard below a woman is kneading dough for bread.

Look here - what's the idea of having Sahathor come to me with old dried-up barley from Memphis and not giving me my ten sacks in fresh, good barley? So, you're happy, are you, chomping down on good barley while I'm neglected?

Tools of the Trade

Wealthy Egyptians had models of servants made for their tombs to work for them in the Afterlife. The model servant holding a hoe (right) is from the Old Kingdom. Compare his hoe to the actual wooden hoes from the New Kingdom 500 years later (below, right). You can see that the shape never really changed.

Land was prepared for sowing with both hoes and ploughs. A wooden plough of the New Kingdom is shown below. This one was hand-held, but the Egyptians also used teams of oxen or donkeys to plough fields. Farmers harvested their crops by hand using sickles like these.

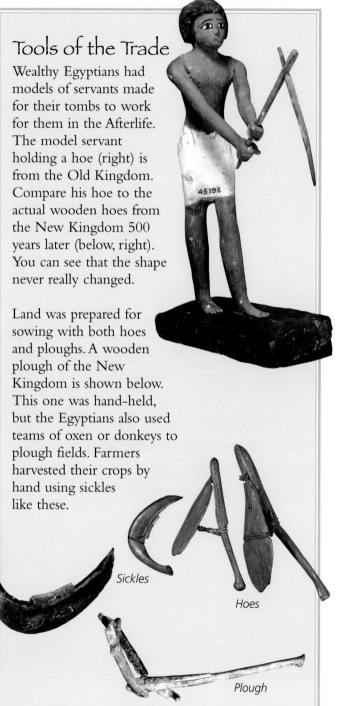

Sickles

Hoes

Plough

The Cycle of Life

The ideal harvest relied upon a delicate balance. Every year, the Egyptians anxiously awaited the coming of the Inundation, when the Nile flooded its banks. Agriculture completely depended on the rich, black silt the river carried with it and left on the banks when it overflowed. If the waters were too low, the flood would not cover the banks and the fertilizing silt would never reach the fields. If the waters were too high, the river could destroy houses and might strip away the silt again when it receded. Without deposits of the silt, Egypt was just a desert and nothing could grow. You can clearly see the line even in modern Egypt where the fertile fields meet the dry desert.

The river's height was carefully measured and recorded at points throughout the country as the waters began to rise at the end of June.

The Nilometer at Elephantine Island. Officials watched how long it took for the water to cover the steps, and could tell how high the Nile flood would be that year.

If the balance was right, as soon as the waters ebbed away around October, the ground could be ploughed to make it ready for planting. Crops were ready to harvest around March. The most important crops were barley and emmer-wheat, which were used to make bread and beer. In Egypt everyone drank beer, including children.

Beer was made from barley baked into loaves which were soaked with mashed grain. Once the mixture had fermented, it was poured through sieves into jars. It could be brewed to different strengths – a lighter, weaker brew for everyday drinking and a stronger, darker brew for special occasions.

The Egyptians also grew grapes, although wine was a luxury. This painting shows wine jars in stands, draped with bunches of grapes.

Baking Bread

The Egyptians were expert bakers. We know that they made dozens of types of loaves and cakes in different shapes and sizes. This triangle-shaped loaf (right) was baked around 1500 BC.

We know that a lot of grit was baked into bread by accident. The teeth of mummies from ancient Egypt are badly worn down because of this.

There were many stages in preparing grain both for baking bread and making beer. This model comes from the tomb of King Montuhotep II and shows dozens of servants grinding grain and getting it ready for the ovens behind them. Meanwhile, an overseer walks between them to make sure they are working hard.

Tomb model of two servants making bread. One grinds the grain and the other bakes the loaves.

A Hard Life

Wealthy boys learning to read and write copied out school texts full of stern warnings about how awful all other jobs could be. Being a farmer was one of the worst! It was described as constant toil throughout the day and into the night, protecting plough-animals from jackals, sowing seed only to have it gobbled up by snakes, and being beaten when you could not pay your taxes.

Usually, everyone had to pay part of their harvest in tax, usually around 10 per cent. Tombs of the Old Kingdom are filled with images of beatings dealt out to those unable or unwilling to pay their taxes (left).

Life was hard for farmers and herdsmen even without beatings. It is curious that in Egyptian art most Egyptians are pictured as ideal - never old, never ugly, always composed and dignified. Yet servants who work the land are often shown with imperfections and flaws. We see elderly herdsmen with balding heads and twisted legs, and farmers with humped backs. Those who worked in the water, either fishing or herding cattle across streams, are sometimes shown with lumps on their bodies, a sign that they have been in infected water. Maybe the idea was to make it clear to the observer that these servants worked so hard for their masters that it showed on their bodies.

A stooped and balding herdsman, painted in the tomb of Nebamun.

Tending Animals

The Egyptians thought of cattle as the most important domestic animals. Cattle were kept in herds by both private owners and by big state and temple estates. Oxen were sacrificed as special offerings to the gods and to the dead. For most people meat was a luxury item rather than a daily food.

Cattle from Nebamun's estate. Each one is painted a different colour.

The Egyptians also kept various types of birds, goats and sheep. Herdsmen and field workers sometimes hunted hares or gazelles from the desert. Sometimes servants are shown fattening rather unusual animals for slaughter. In the tomb of Mereruka, the vizier and son-in-law of King Teti of the 6th Dynasty, hyenas are being force-fed (below).

Model showing the preparation of food and drink. Cows are often shown being slaughtered for meat, but the Egyptians did eat other animals.

A funerary feast in the making. The servants of the nobleman Sebekaa present him with live animals from his estate, including geese, a goat and a large ox, that will sustain him in his Afterlife. He is shown receiving a foreleg, a symbol of strength, and inspecting the animals.

Animal Magic!

The most important duty of any herdsman was to keep his animals safe. He had to keep birds of prey, from falcons to crows, away from young animals which they could easily steal away in their talons. Predators such as jackals were a danger to all, especially at night. A governor named Henku proudly states in his tomb that he

... fed the jackals of the mountain and the kites of the sky with the hides of sheep and goats ...

to keep his people and their animals safe. Crocodiles were a danger to sheep and cattle grazing near the river. Herdsmen had to be watchful at all times – but they also tried using magic to keep their animals safe. There were spells to 'close the mouths' of predatory animals like jackals and wolves, and to keep crocodiles away from cattle. One unusual spell of this type is written in a papyrus full of medical remedies. It is to be spoken as a scarecrow is set up. It is our only evidence that the Egyptians used scarecrows:

(A spell) for stopping a bird of prey from snatching:
(Take) an acacia branch and set it standing. Then a man should say: 'Horus – he has been scavenging in the town and in the country! His appetite should be confined to the territory of birds. Let him cook! Let him eat!'
Spell to be said over an acacia branch upon which a cake has been placed. This is the way to stop a bird of prey from snatching.

6 Builders and Craftsmen

The ones who built in granite, who crafted halls in fine tombs of perfect construction – after the ones who commissioned them have become gods, their own offering stones have fallen into ruin ...

'The Dispute of a Man with his Soul', Middle Kingdom.

Finely-carved hieroglyphs from Dendera temple showing the craftsman god Khnum using his potter's wheel, and a builder grinding mortar.

Egyptian builders and craftsmen were famous for their attention to detail and their love of beauty, which can be seen both in their colossal monuments and in the smallest objects. Many people were involved in creating every building and piece of art, from a pyramid to a wall painting. We know little about the craftsmen themselves, because the glory of what they created went to those who paid for it.

Still, certain details of their art and sometimes their lives do survive if we look in the right places. In this chapter, we go in search of Egypt's master craftsmen by looking at their works, how they created them and the tools they used.

The stela of the craftsman Iunna, showing him worshipping the boat he built.

Quarrying and Building

The pyramids of Giza and the huge temple complex of Karnak display the Egyptians' skill in building with stone. There were two kinds of buildings in ancient Egypt – those that were free-standing and those that were carved into a living rock-face. The building materials for any free-standing structure had to be quarried.

The Egyptians had a wide choice of stones. The most popular materials were limestone and granite. Limestone was easy to find; the blocks that were used for the Giza pyramids came from the nearby quarries of Tura and from the Giza plateau itself.

Granite came only from the area around Aswan, in the south of Egypt. Quarrying and working granite was a tough job because the stone was so hard. The Egyptians split sheets of granite along carefully measured lines by using wedges made of wood. They made the wedges expand by using water. Sometimes the rock cracked in the wrong place and the whole process had to start over again.

The Egyptians also quarried other types of stone, such as alabaster and gneiss, for decoration and for statues. Many people must have died on quarrying missions which ventured deep into Egypt's burning-hot deserts, where food and water were scarce. Those who survived left graffiti on the quarry walls for other quarriers:

As for anyone who will salute my image here, may he reach his home safely once he's done what he came here to do!

The pyramids of Khufu and Khafre at Giza. The blocks of stone that make up the inner layer of the pyramid of Khufu are roughly hewn, in contrast to the smooth casing blocks that you can still see at the top of Khafre's pyramid.

The alabaster quarry at Hatnub. Left, an alabaster statue of a noblewoman of the 5th Dynasty.

Once the stone for a free-standing building had been quarried, it had to be moved to the building site. This was often a monumental task in itself, particularly in the case of granite. Granite blocks usually had to be carried down to the river Nile so that they could be transported in large boats.

Each block of stone in the Giza pyramids weighs on average 2.5 tonnes. It must have been a massive undertaking to put just one of the giant stones in place. There were about 2,300,000 of these blocks altogether in the Great Pyramid, and that is not counting the granite beams inside the pyramid or the basalt flooring outside it. The builders made massive ramps of mud bricks to allow the stone blocks to be dragged into position. When the building work was finished, these ramps were dismantled. Only a few examples survive from building projects that were left unfinished - for example, the entrance gateway of Karnak temple, called the First Pylon (below).

Remains of the mud-brick ramp used by the builders of the First Pylon at Karnak temple, Thebes.

Calculations and Planning

Mathematics must have played an important role in all crafts, especially in building something like a pyramid. It might look funny, or even fall down, if its size and slope were not carefully calculated! One mathematical papyrus says:

Accurate computation is the gateway to knowledge of all things and of dark mysteries!

Egyptian artists measured out the figures they painted. We have evidence of guidelines on walls which allowed the artist – or more commonly, a team of artists working together – to place figures and texts on a wall before completing their details (right).

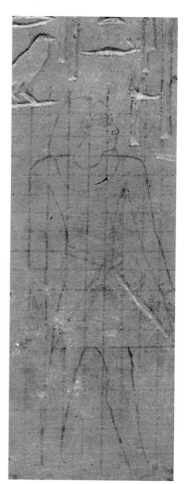

The grids let artists produce figures with consistent proportions. A standing figure was divided into 18 squares, so that the soles of his/her feet rested on the bottom line of the first square, and his/her hairline formed the top line of the last square.

Only important figures such as kings or noblemen were depicted in this strict way. Lesser figures, such as servants or workmen, were drawn freehand.

A master draughtsman would inspect all the rough sketches – always made in red – and make any corrections necessary before the lines were drawn in more solidly in black. The next stage would be carving – either in sunken relief (cutting away the inside of images) or raised relief (cutting away the background to make images stand out). Then the wall would be painted. Grid-lines were supposed to be removed by the process of sculpting and painting, but since many tomb walls and stelae were left unfinished, they remain for us to see (below).

Draughtman's sketches on an ostracon (flake of pottery) in red and black ink.

Unfinished limestone stela of the sculptor Userwer. One of the unfinished figures, with its grid-lines, is shown on page 46.

Sculpting

The same craftsmen who carved out figures on tomb walls and stelae probably also carved free-standing statues. Many of the same techniques were used. Any statue started as a block of stone, on to which grid-lines were drawn to guide the sculptor in his cutting. Again, it is likely that teams of sculptors worked on statues – this is suggested by images in tombs showing statues of the tomb-owner being made. Sculpting could be a very important task. One official of the Middle Kingdom tells us on his stela that the king asked him to have new cult images of the gods of Abydos sculpted. The word for 'to be sculpted' literally means 'to be born'. Divine statues like this were made for temples, where they served as houses for a god's spirit and therefore ultimately *became* the god. Creating them must have felt like an enormous honour for a sculptor.

Of course, sculptors carved colossal works as well as smaller-scale statues. Imagine how the sculptors who carved the twenty-metre-high statues of King Ramses II from the living rock at Abu Simbel must have felt, watching the features of their king take shape beneath their chisels!

One of four huge statues of Ramses II at Abu Simbel, his finest temple in Nubia.

Tools of the Trade

Certain tools were used by more than one type of craftsman. The group of tools below was found together in a basket placed in a tomb in Thebes. The tools probably belonged to a carpenter, who wanted to take the symbols of his craft into the Afterlife.

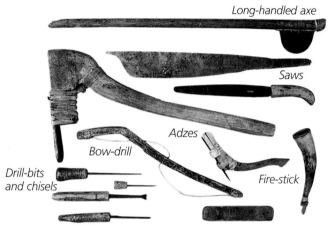

Long-handled axe

Saws

Adzes

Bow-drill

Drill-bits and chisels

Fire-stick

The people involved in the building of a tomb were often the same people who tried to rob it, and so overseers kept a careful watch on workmen and the tools they used. At the Valley of the Kings, overseers took special care of three things: wicks from lamps, copper chisels and wooden mallets. With those three tools, a workman could break into a tomb and rob it.

Wooden mallet.

Granite statue of the ship-builder Ankhwa, who holds an adze in his left hand – the typical tool of his trade. The inscription on his lap tells us he was also a smith.

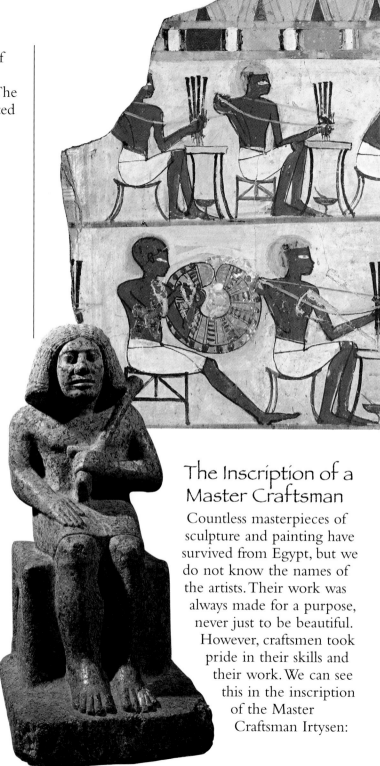

The Inscription of a Master Craftsman

Countless masterpieces of sculpture and painting have survived from Egypt, but we do not know the names of the artists. Their work was always made for a purpose, never just to be beautiful. However, craftsmen took pride in their skills and their work. We can see this in the inscription of the Master Craftsman Irtysen:

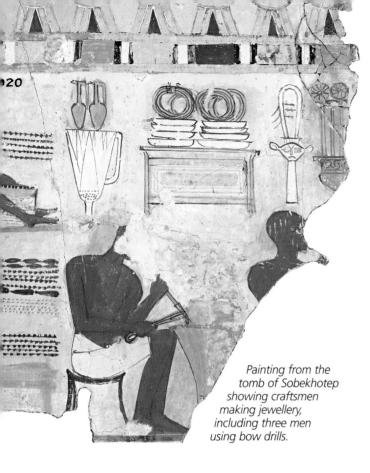

Painting from the tomb of Sobekhotep showing craftsmen making jewellery, including three men using bow drills.

One part of his inscription stands out. This describes the delicate balance of his skills, which allows him to represent both tiny details of a composition and the broader picture perfectly. They sound very like a poem:

I know the outgoings of male figures,
and the recessings of female figures;
the uprightness of many birds of prey,
and the cringing of a single captive;
the glancing of one eye in harmony with the other,
and the growing fear on the face of victims.

Stela (carved stone) telling the life-story of the master craftsman Irtysen.

I am truly a craftsman, talented in his craft, who emerged as the authority in his area. I understand the phases of the water's recession, the balance of calculations, the process of hollowing out and inserting (a piece) - that is, its exit and entry points - so that a part moves into its place. I know how to make pigments and substances that we can apply without heating them in fire, that we need not soak in water either. No man will ever excel in these skills except me! I am unique, together with my eldest son of my body.

Ironically, we cannot point to a single piece of painting or sculpture that Irtysen made. Yet the pride that craftsmen like Irtysen took in their work is obvious in the perfect lines of the works of art they created. Even if their names are lost, their legacy remains.

Coloured minerals like these were ground on a hard stone to make paint. According to Irtysen, every craftsman had his own special recipe.

7 Soldiers and Conquerors

*The name of the brave man
is in his deeds – it will never
ever perish in the land.*

Inscription of Ahmose, 18th Dynasty.

Throughout Egyptian history
there were many kings who
wanted to be remembered as great
warriors. Soldiers must have played an
important role in these kings'
conquests, especially during the New
Kingdom when the Egyptian empire
was being forged through war. But in
art and texts the soldiers are always
overshadowed by the king. It is
always the colossal figure of the king
who dominates the scenes of battle
carved onto temple walls and
always the king who single-
handedly defeats his enemy in
the accompanying texts. His
soldiers are often just part of
the background. In this chapter, we
find out what was life really like for
these men who helped the king to
win his victories.

*A nobleman's bodyguard
holding a huge shield and
a long-handled axe.*

Soldiers' Training and Experiences

From the New Kingdom on, there were professional soldiers who spent their lives serving in the king's army and navy. Before that, the king simply gathered his army from the towns and villages. Anyone could be called into service. School exercises from the New Kingdom describe how awful a soldier's life could be, compared to that of a scribe:

If only you'd concentrate on writing as hard as you can! – don't let your hand stop. Look at what the king does. All his plans are harsh! All his subjects are registered and the best ones among them are snatched away. The grown man is made to be a soldier; the youth to be a warrior; and as for the little boy, they take him right out of his mother's arms. When he grows into a man, his bones are doddery. Are you a donkey? You'll be tamed! There'll be no spirit in your body!

Before the New Kingdom, even the men who commanded armies were not trained soldiers. A man named Weni who lived in the early 6th Dynasty spent most of his career as an administrator. But the king asked him five times to command his army on campaigns into Asia. In his tomb, Weni tells us that he strictly supervised his men's behaviour:

... so that no one attacked his companion, or seized a loaf or sandals from a passer-by, or stole a cloth from any town, or pinched a goat from anyone.

Soldiers practising their skills by hunting wild animals in the desert, carved on a palette of the Predynastic Period.

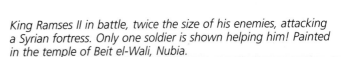

King Ramses II in battle, twice the size of his enemies, attacking a Syrian fortress. Only one soldier is shown helping him! Painted in the temple of Beit el-Wali, Nubia.

Some of the most detailed images of the experiences of soldiers come from the 18th Dynasty tomb of King Horemhab at Saqqara. He started to build it before he became king. Horemhab had many military titles, including 'Great Commander of the Army for the Lord of the Two Lands' which he held under Tutankhamun. He was a soldier himself, so he recorded the duties of his men with a lot of care.

Some scenes show unusual detail and even a sense of humour – like this one in which an Egyptian soldier tells off a much bigger, mean-looking Nubian captive.

Scenes from Horemhab's tomb showing his soldiers gathering supplies and preparing the general's tent.

A City Under Siege

A soldier named Inti from Dishasha was so proud of conquering a walled Syrian town that he had the details carved on a wall of his tomb (a drawing of it is shown below). The Syrian town is on the right inside oval walls. You can see the chief on the second line from the top. He holds his head in his hands as a weeping woman tells him that the city is doomed.

Outside the city walls, the fighting is fierce. Some Egyptian soldiers are climbing up a ladder to get over the city wall, while others batter the foundations with long staffs. To the left, Egyptian soldiers grab their enemies by the hair and threaten them with swords. Most of the Syrians have been struck by arrows, but the Egyptians are all unhurt.

At the bottom left, you can see a line of captives, including women and children, being led away. Can you spot the Syrian woman slung over an Egyptian soldier's shoulder? The man in front has turned, maybe to catch one last glimpse of his home.

Soldiers' Duties

Soldiers were not called up only for war. They sometimes went with expeditions to the deserts of Egypt, Nubia and the Sinai to quarry stone. This could be just as dangerous for soldiers as fighting, because they had to work in great heat with only limited supplies of food and water.

Soldiers also went to fortresses in Nubia, especially in the Middle Kingdom when strings of forts were built between the first and second cataracts (where rocks blocked the river Nile).

View of the massive walls of the fortress at Buhen in Nubia. Every Nubian fortress was unique in design, protected by thick mud-brick walls and ditches. Buhen's granaries could provide food for several hundred men.

Many of the garrison soldiers lived out their lives far away from home. Perhaps some tried to run away or to avoid being called for duty at all. In the Middle Kingdom, we hear of establishments like prisons to punish men and women who tried to escape their duties to the king.

The stela of Kay, who is shown armed with a bow and arrows. He was an Overseer of Desert Huntsmen in the Middle Kingdom. Kay describes searching the western oases for tracks and bringing back any fugitives he found there so that his forces were 'complete'. He calls himself a loyal servant of the king, saying: 'What was commanded of me came off successfully.'

Soldiers and the King

It was through their relationship with the king that many soldiers, especially in the New Kingdom, distinguished themselves and rose high within the ranks of society. One of the best examples is a man named Ahmose, who fought in the wars against the Hyksos in the early 18th Dynasty. He began his career as a humble member of the crew of one of the king's ships. His bravery brought him to the attention of the king, who promoted him and rewarded him with gold and slaves for his part in the capture of the Hyksos capital Avaris. The words quoted at the beginning of the chapter are from his tomb at el-Kab.

Horse-drawn chariot on the estate of the nobleman Nebamun. Chariots such as this were a sign of high status.

In the New Kingdom, gold flies like these were awarded for bravery. It is a mystery why the Egyptians chose the fly shape.

At the end of his long career, Ahmose had served three kings and had been awarded the gold of honour – a special reward for outstanding service to the king – seven times, as well as gifts of slaves and land. But he was proudest of his reputation, and was confident that long after his death, his name would survive. And so it has.

Types of Soldier

There were a few special groups of soldiers. The men of the chariot division were the highest-ranking soldiers in the Egyptian army. The Egyptians learned how to make and use chariots in the early 18th Dynasty. Soon the chariot became associated with the king. In the New Kingdom, the king is often shown shooting arrows at his enemies from his chariot.

The Egyptians sometimes took foreign soldiers into their armies. Many of these foreigners were captured in battle and then forced to fight for the Egyptian king. However, some were paid mercenaries, like the Nubian archers who served in the Egyptian army from the end of the Old Kingdom onwards.

In the New Kingdom, Asiatic soldiers known as the *Maryannu* and the *Na'arn* were prized as skilled charioteers. King Amenhotep II boasts of capturing 550 *Maryannu* warriors after a battle. A group of Mediterranean nomads known as the *Sherden* were fierce spearmen. In battle scenes, the Sherden stand out from all the other soldiers because of their distinctive helmets (below).

Group of Sherden mercenaries, wearing their horned helmets. They are carved on a wall of Medinet Habu temple at Thebes.

Casualties of War

Soldiers who fought for their king were promised great rewards and became wealthy men. But we know very little about what happened when a battle was lost, because the Egyptians never admitted any of their defeats. King Ramses II spent most of his life boasting of his great victory over the Hittites at Qadesh. In actual fact, we know (from Hittite accounts of the battle!) that Ramses was nearly killed after his men deserted him.

Similarly, Egypt suffered terrible defeats in the reign of the Nubian king Taharqa – but we only know of them from Assyrian descriptions. King Esarhaddon of Assyria reports happily that in battle he struck Taharqa five times with his arrows. Esarhaddon's son, Ashurbanipal, invaded Egypt again a few years later. Again Taharqa was defeated and this time had to run for his life. Ashurbanipal decorated the walls of his palace with scenes of his victory over the Egyptians (see below).

Defeated enemies of King Montuhotep II, from his temple at Deir el-Bahri in Thebes.

What happened to Egyptians who died in battle? One group of soldiers was honoured with a special tomb. It was built near the temple of King Montuhotep II and it is likely that the men buried inside it were his soldiers. Some of the bodies are still pierced with the arrows that killed them. Others look as if they have been battered with heavy stones. All had been attacked by crows or vultures. The bodies must have been a powerful reminder of the harsh realities of war.

A rare image of the Egyptians under attack. This scene from the Assyrian king Ashurbanipal's palace shows the Assyrians attacking a fortified Egyptian city and carrying away captives in the 7th century BC.

Ancient Egyptian Weapons

Many local governors in the First Intermediate Period and early Middle Kingdom controlled their own armies. The scene below comes from the tomb of Djehutyhotep, a Middle Kingdom governor of Bersha, and shows his soldiers protecting his property. Many examples of the weapons they carry still survive today.

Soldier armed with an axe like this one (right) and a cow-hide shield.

Soldiers armed with long spears.

Bronze spear blade found in a tomb at Abydos.

A soldier carrying a spear and wearing a breastplate bound to his chest by strips of linen. Soldiers in the New Kingdom sometimes wore a kilt with protective netting (right).

Bow made from acacia wood, with reed arrows. Three arrows have flint points. They were buried in the tomb of a man called Ankhef at Asyut.

Soldier with bow and arrows leads the group.

8 Musicians and Dancers

Don't let your heart break over all
that which may happen.
Put music all around you!
Don't dwell on dark thoughts,
which the god hates.
Remember happiness!

'Harper's Song' from the Tomb of Inherkhau,
20th Dynasty.

The Egyptians celebrated life and mourned death with music and dance. We find images of entertainers in both temples and tombs throughout Egyptian history. Music could be connected with religion, but it was also part of everyday life. Field workers and fisherman sang simple songs as they worked and the words were sometimes carved alongside them on tomb walls. Everyone wanted to take music with them into the Afterlife.

Colourful images survive of the men and women who worked as entertainers. Many paintings, like the one opposite, show us music and dance being performed. We even have some ancient Egyptian musical instruments. In this chapter, we meet the entertainers.

Entertainment in Tombs

Nebamun was an official in the 18th Dynasty. His tomb at Thebes is now lost, but parts of its decoration survive. Several fragments, like the one opposite, show a splendid banquet. In the top half of the scene, the guests are served food and drink. They wear cones of incense on their heads and hold sweet-smelling lotus flowers to their noses.

The entertainers are shown below. The two dancing girls just wear belts around their waists like the serving-girl, but they have all sorts of jewellery that jingled as they moved. Beside them, one woman plays a double oboe and three others clap in time. We know the musicians are singing because the words of their song are written above their heads. Their song is about the simple beauty of flowers growing and the pleasure of their scent. The four musicians wear flowing robes and heavy jewellery, just like the lady guests above them. They also have cones of incense on their heads. But can you see the differences between the entertainers and the guests?

The guests at the banquet have their heads turned to the side and their feet on the ground. But below, two of the entertainers are shown full-faced. We also see the soles of the musicians' feet, because they sit with their legs tucked underneath them. The bodies of the guests overlap a little, but look at the two dancers!

One dancer has interlaced the fingers of her hands, and her legs twine around the other dancer's leg. All the usual rules of Egyptian art do not apply to entertainers.

Cones of incense are painted on the guests' heads to show that their hair has been scented. In real life, such cones would be very uncomfortable to wear.

The Beautiful Festival of the Valley

If we had all the pieces of the scene on page 59, we would probably see a large figure of the tomb-owner, Nebamun, sitting facing his guests and their entertainers. Egyptologists think that scenes like this show the Beautiful Festival of the Valley, one of the most important events in Thebes. During this festival, priests took a statue of the god Amun from Karnak temple to visit the royal temples on the West Bank of the Nile. At the same time, the people of Thebes visited the tombs of their relatives on the West Bank. They brought food and drink offerings for them and feasted in special rooms in the tombs. In this way, the living and the dead always celebrated the festival together. The guests in the scene from Nebamun's tomb are probably members of his family. The entertainers could also be family.

Musicians

Another fragment of painting from Nebamun's tomb shows a second group of entertainers (right). These musicians are dressed like the other entertainers above – with flowing robes, golden jewellery, and incense cones.

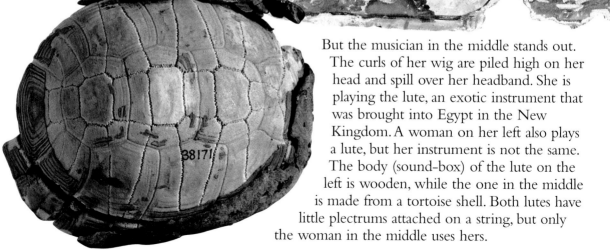

A lute made from a tortoise shell. Its strings and handle are now missing. Holes were cut into the shell to deepen its sound.

But the musician in the middle stands out. The curls of her wig are piled high on her head and spill over her headband. She is playing the lute, an exotic instrument that was brought into Egypt in the New Kingdom. A woman on her left also plays a lute, but her instrument is not the same. The body (sound-box) of the lute on the left is wooden, while the one in the middle is made from a tortoise shell. Both lutes have little plectrums attached on a string, but only the woman in the middle uses hers.

The woman in between the two lute-players claps her hands to set a rhythm for the musicians. To the right of the central figure, one woman plays a double oboe and another woman beats a tambourine. Some of the group may be singing, but this time the words of their song are not written above them.

Music and the Gods

Music and dance were also used to entertain the gods. Certain gods had a special connection with music, especially Hathor, the goddess of love. A special dance was performed for her by women. They held their arms above their heads to mimic the shape of the horns of Hathor's sacred animal, the cow.

A female dancer performing the 'cow-dance' in the tomb of Werirenptah.

A type of rattle known as a sistrum was sacred to Hathor. The sistrum could either be looped at the top or shaped like a little shrine (*naos*). The Egyptians worshipped other gods with the sound of the sistrum. The lady Anhai, who lived in the 20th Dynasty in Thebes, is shown holding a loop-shaped sistrum in the papyrus that was buried in her tomb (right). Her title is 'songstress of the god Amun'.

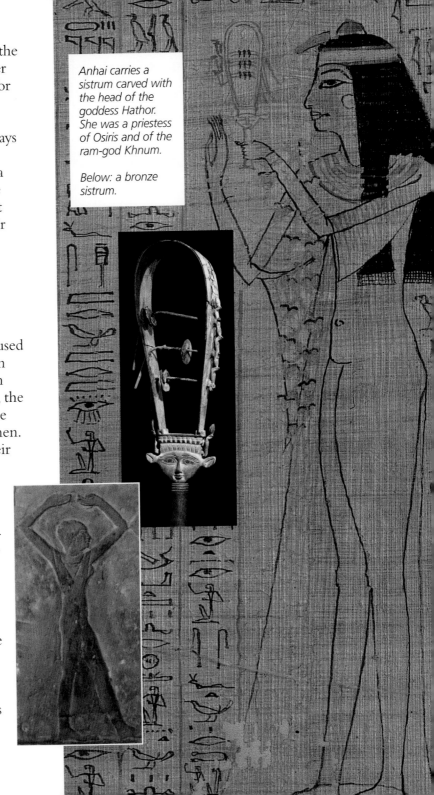

Anhai carries a sistrum carved with the head of the goddess Hathor. She was a priestess of Osiris and of the ram-god Khnum.

Below: a bronze sistrum.

Special Entertainers

Some entertainers performed in their home-town for their families or for their local gods, but there were also travelling musicians. 'The Tales of Wonder' tells the story of the birth of three kings of the 5th Dynasty whose father is the sun-god Re.

The stela of Mahu with a solo harpist at the top.

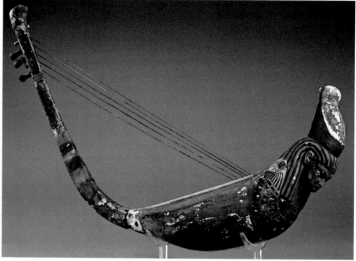

A New Kingdom model harp.

Re sends four goddesses who know all about childbirth to help the kings' mother. The goddesses disguise themselves as travelling musicians, taking along the ram-headed god Khnum as their porter. In this disguise, they are welcomed into the house and they are rewarded afterwards with a sack of grain.

Certain entertainers were especially important, like the harpist. Women sometimes played the harp in groups, but only male harpists were shown alone on stelae (tomb-stones), like the one on the left, and on tomb walls from the Old Kingdom onwards. The Harper's Songs they sang were often about the sadness of death. Some painted very gloomy pictures of the Afterlife. They called the realm of the dead 'the silent land, from which no one ever comes back' and they urged men and women to fill their lives with as much happiness as they could. Most solo harpists seem to have been blind. Perhaps because they could not see the world around them, they had a special insight into the next world.

This figurine shows the fierce dwarf-god Bes making loud music with a drum or a tambourine.

Another special entertainer was the dancing dwarf. The most famous is the god Bes (above). He used his wild looks and loud music to scare away evil spirits from children and their mothers.

The musicians and dancers who entertained the gods, kings and people of ancient Egypt always had a special importance because of the delight they inspired. We can see this even in the Egyptian script. In hieroglyphs, dancing figures were used to write the words for 'joy' and 'celebration'!

The King's Entertainer

A very famous dwarf is mentioned in a letter from King Pepi II of the 6th Dynasty to one of his officials, named Harkhuf. Harkhuf had just returned from an expedition far beyond Egypt's southern borders and he was bringing all sorts of exotic treasure back for his king. Pepi II ruled Egypt for more than ninety years, but when he wrote to Harkhuf, he was just a young boy. He was desperate to see the dwarf Harkhuf was bringing back with him:

Sail north to the palace immediately! Hurry! Bring with you this dwarf – alive, safe and sound – whom you have taken from the land of the Horizon-dwellers for the dances of the gods, to delight the senses, to lift the spirits of the King of Upper and Lower Egypt, Neferkare, who lives forever. When he goes down with you into your boat, make sure trustworthy people are around him on both sides of the boat. Be careful that he does not fall into the water! When he sleeps at night, again make sure that trustworthy people sleep all around him in his tent. Check on him ten times a night! My majesty longs to see this dwarf more than the treasures of the Mine-Land and Punt!

Harkhuf was so delighted with his letter from the king that he had a copy of it carved into the outside wall of his tomb at Aswan.

9 Foreigners and Travellers

A savage lion can calm his fury and start
to be like a tame donkey.
A horse can accept its harness and be
obedient when it goes out.
This dog here obeys commands and
follows its master.
A monkey can carry a stick, though its
mother did not carry one.
A goose can return from the watering-hole
when someone comes to shut it into the yard.
You can teach Nubians to speak Egyptian
– Syrians and other foreigners too!
Say: 'I will do as all the animals do.'
Listen and you can learn what they have.

'Instructions of Ani', New Kingdom.

Fragment of painting from the tomb
of the nobleman Sobekhotep,
showing a Syrian bringing precious
gifts and horses to the king.

The Egyptians felt proud of who they
were. They saw Egypt as the land of
civilization. The Nile provided them with
easy transport, and each year its flood-
waters brought them the fertile silt that
made farming possible. Yet the Egyptians
also mingled with foreign peoples, both
trading with them and fighting them for
control of territory. The Egyptians believed
they were better than any foreigners. But
what happened when foreign powers got
uncomfortably close to home? In this chapter,
we explore the Egyptians' attitude towards
foreigners, both at home and abroad.

Boundaries

Natural boundaries surrounded Egypt: the Mediterranean Sea lay to the north, deserts to the east and west, and a series of rocky barriers, called cataracts, blocked the Nile in the south. The Egyptians thought of any place beyond these boundaries as rough, foreign territory.

In hieroglyphs, the names of all Egyptian cities ended with a little round sign with two crossed lines inside: ⊗. It represented a walled city with two perfectly straight streets running through it and was a symbol of order. By contrast, the names of all foreign places in hieroglyphs ended with the desert hills hieroglyph: ᨉ – a symbol of chaos. Even foreign cities swallowed up by the Egyptian empire were still written with the ᨉ sign.

Egypt called all of its foreign neighbours 'the Nine Bows' – the bow being a symbol of hostility. If you look at the feet of statues of Egyptian kings, you will often see nine bows carved under their sandals. This quietly suggested that the king was always on top of his enemies.

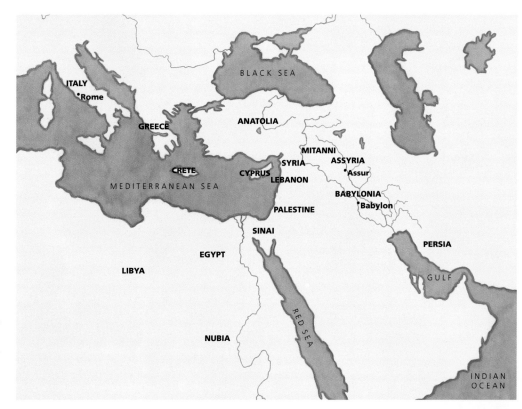

This map shows the kingdoms of the foreign peoples who surrounded Egypt. Some, like the Mitanni, became friendly with Egypt. Others, like the Assyrians, were always enemies.

Foreigners as Captives

In times of war, Egypt was merciless towards its enemies. At the beginning of the 18th Dynasty, King Thutmosis I carved a long inscription into the rock face at Tumbus in Nubia to commemorate the territory he had won in the second year of his reign. His inscription describes in cruel detail what happened to the Nubians who stood in his way:

Their guts flooded their valleys, the gore from their mouths poured like torrents of rain. The scavenger birds upon them were countless as they swooped down and carried them off to other places, and the crocodile seized anyone who tried to escape ...

War brought many foreigners into Egypt. Thousands of captives were put to work in Egypt, or forced to join the Egyptian army. Captives who became slaves were often given Egypian names by their new owners.

Wall tile from the palace of King Ramses III, showing a bound Libyan captive.

King Ramses II carved lists of all the cities he captured in battle. The cities are all shown as bound captives, whose bodies are fortress signs with their names inside. Each has the foreign city sign.

This Roman lady lived in Egypt and was mummified in the Egyptian style. This portrait was found on her coffin.

Foreign Settlers in Egypt

Many foreigners came to Egypt willingly. Some were messengers bringing greetings or demands from foreign kings. Others were traders, selling exotic food, drink and other wares. The word for 'haggling' in Egyptian literally means 'to do business in the Syrian tongue'! Some visitors decided to stay permanently. Egypt must have seemed like a land of opportunity. We know that many different races of people lived in Egypt by the time of the New Kingdom – Asiatics from Syria, Palestine, Anatolia and Babylonia, Libyans from the west who settled in colonies in the Delta, and Nubians who gradually established settlements in the south around Elephantine Island. Sometimes there are only subtle clues to tell us that they were not actually Egyptian. Some men and women had foreign names, but were shown as Egyptians in traditionally Egyptian dress. By contrast, others who had Egyptian names were shown with foreign features – like Syrian men with pointed beards or Nubian women with bare chests who wore only wraparound skirts.

Often foreign parents gave their children Egyptian names – perhaps to help them 'blend in'. But others seem to have been proud of their origins, especially the Nubian mercenaries who lived in Gebelein in the First Intermediate Period. One named Qedes freely acknowledges that he is a 'Nehesy' – a Nubian. He also boasts (in true Egyptian fashion!) that he is faster than anyone in his town, Nubians and Egyptians alike. The funerary prayers on his stela are purely Egyptian.

Stela of the Nubian mercenary Qedes. His mother, Ibeb, stands beside him, and his Egyptian servant presents him with a drink.

Foreigners Bringing Tribute

Many tombs show scenes of foreign rulers bringing precious and exotic gifts to the king. The Egyptians expected all lands under their control to bring this tribute once a year. In return, the king granted the people 'the breath of life'.

This scene from the tomb of Menkheperresoneb shows the ruler of Crete kissing the ground before the king, while the Hittite king raises his arms in praise. The two Syrian rulers behind him carry gifts of silver, gold, turquoise and minerals.

This similar scene is from the tomb of the treasurer Sobekhotep. It was his job to collect tribute for King Thutmosis IV. The men are bringing gold, ivory and wine.

Children are often shown in tribute scenes. The Egyptians insisted that the sons and daughters of foreign rulers be brought to Egypt to be educated. That way the king made sure that they grew up into friends rather than enemies. Many of them used their title 'Child of the Royal Nursery' with pride. The shipwright Iunna used it 12 times on his stela!

These hieroglyphs say: 'Child of the Royal Nursery, the king's beloved one, Iunna'.

Egyptians Abroad

Sometimes, the king sent trusted officials on missions abroad. King Thutmosis III sent Sennefer to Lebanon to bring back timber for the temple of Amun at Karnak. The account of Sennefer's journey 'across the Great Green' (the Mediterranean Sea) tells how he walked into the cedar forest in a rainstorm. While he chose trees for timber, Sennefer politely honoured the goddess of the mountain:

I made sure that gifts of millions of things were presented to her on your behalf, Majesty (life, health, prosperity to you!).

It was a hard journey for Sennefer. He says, 'it was sharper than an ear of corn!' Most Egyptians felt the same way about leaving home. Soldiers and miners had to stay away from home for a long time, so they tried to surround themselves with reminders of home. Very often they worshipped the goddess of love and happiness, Hathor, who was a mother figure for the lonely. She had shrines in Nubia, the Sinai and in Syria.

Sandstone sphinx made by miners working in Sinai to honour the goddess Hathor. Her name is written on its shoulder.

The fierce storm-god Seth was linked with foreigners and was a favourite of the Asiatic Hyksos kings.

Foreign Pharaohs

From time to time, foreign kings sat on the Egyptian throne. The Egyptians were never very happy about this and generally told terrible stories about them. We know, for example, that the Asiatic Hyksos kings, who ruled the north of Egypt after the collapse of the Middle Kingdom, did many good things. They established valuable trading routes, they built many temples to Egyptian gods (especially Seth, left) and they introduced into Egypt the most important weapon of the New Kingdom – the horse and chariot. Yet, when King Ahmose of the 18th Dynasty chased the Hyksos back to Palestine, everyone celebrated.

One of the worst stories was told about the Persian king Cambyses, who ruled Egypt in the 27th Dynasty. People said that he had roasted a sacred Apis bull for a feast! In fact, we know that he tried really hard to be a good king. He took an Egyptian name and worshipped Egyptian gods.

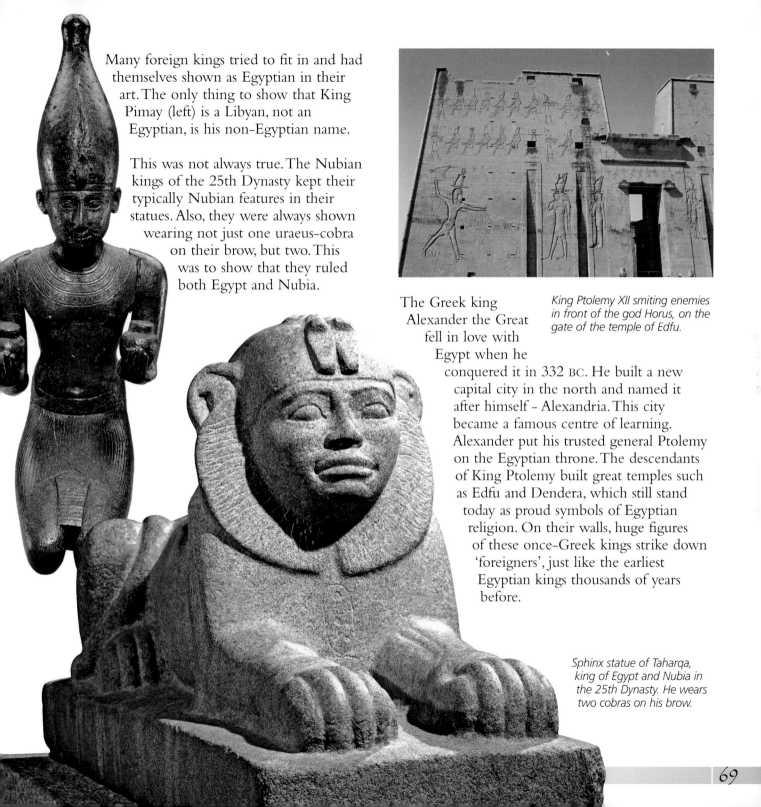

Many foreign kings tried to fit in and had themselves shown as Egyptian in their art. The only thing to show that King Pimay (left) is a Libyan, not an Egyptian, is his non-Egyptian name.

This was not always true. The Nubian kings of the 25th Dynasty kept their typically Nubian features in their statues. Also, they were always shown wearing not just one uraeus-cobra on their brow, but two. This was to show that they ruled both Egypt and Nubia.

King Ptolemy XII smiting enemies in front of the god Horus, on the gate of the temple of Edfu.

The Greek king Alexander the Great fell in love with Egypt when he conquered it in 332 BC. He built a new capital city in the north and named it after himself - Alexandria. This city became a famous centre of learning. Alexander put his trusted general Ptolemy on the Egyptian throne. The descendants of King Ptolemy built great temples such as Edfu and Dendera, which still stand today as proud symbols of Egyptian religion. On their walls, huge figures of these once-Greek kings strike down 'foreigners', just like the earliest Egyptian kings thousands of years before.

Sphinx statue of Taharqa, king of Egypt and Nubia in the 25th Dynasty. He wears two cobras on his brow.

10 Mummies and Mourners

Death seems to me today like the
perfume of myrrh, like sitting under
an awning on a breezy day.
... like the perfume of lotus flowers,
like sitting on the shore of a land of
drunkenness.
... like the clearing of the sky, like the
moment a man grasps all that he did not
understand before.
... like a man's longing to see his home,
after he has spent long years in captivity.

'The Dispute of a Man with his Soul',
Middle Kingdom.

The Egyptians have become famous as
a people obsessed with death. It is
true that kings and their officials began to
prepare their tombs as early as they could.
It is also true that houses for the living
were built mainly with mud-bricks and
wood that have decayed, while more
enduring materials like limestone and
granite were used for tombs and temples.
But there is much more to the story – why
were the Egyptians so focused on their
Afterlife? In this chapter, we will look for
answers to this question by exploring how
the Egyptians prepared for their deaths,
and how this involved the living relatives
they left behind.

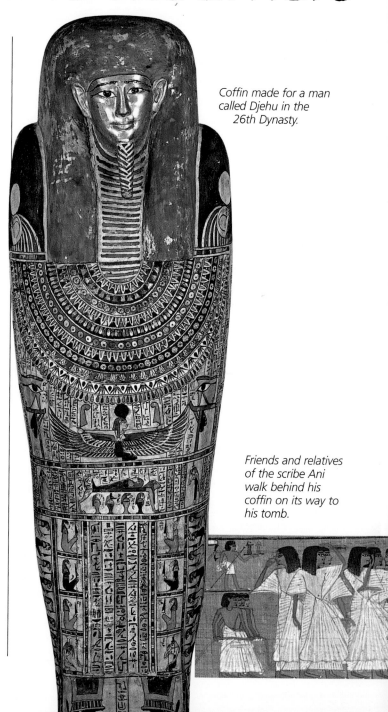

Coffin made for a man called Djehu in the 26th Dynasty.

Friends and relatives of the scribe Ani walk behind his coffin on its way to his tomb.

The Tomb

As soon as they could, wealthy Egyptians began to build a tomb which would be a home for their mummy. But what about those who could not afford a tomb? Did they believe that only the rich could have an Afterlife? Some survived on the tomb walls of their masters, because nobles decorated their tombs with scenes of the people who worked for them. This meant they were destined to work for ever!

The art in tombs was never just a decoration. The Egyptians firmly believed that when they sculpted or painted a person, a thing, a place or even an idea, it magically became real and lasted forever. This is why kings and nobles look strong and perfect on the walls of their tombs and in their statues.

Statue from the tomb of the official Nenkheftka, showing him young and strong.

A tomb with a pyramid-shaped roof standing in the desert. Lotus flowers, a symbol of renewed life, are growing by its entrance. The welcoming mother-goddess Hathor is also shown, in her cow form.

As the tomb was being built and decorated, the funerary equipment would be collected. Wealthy individuals might take all sorts of furniture and fine objects with them. King Tutankhamun's small tomb contained enough items to fill several rooms in the Cairo Museum, though he reigned for only ten years, and was never very powerful as a king. Imagine how much treasure must have been crammed into the tomb of a mighty king such as Ramses II, who reigned for over sixty years.

A Few Facts About Mummification

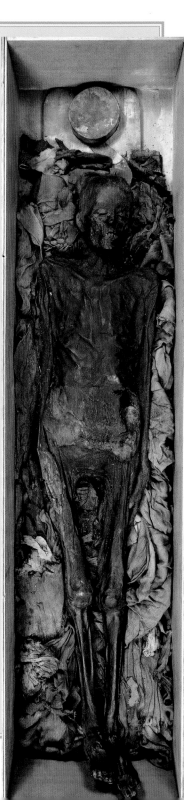

• The Egyptians believed that the jackal-headed god Anubis (left) invented mummification. Priests involved in mummification wore jackal masks.

• The body had to be whole when it was mummified, so if a leg was missing, one would be supplied. There are mummies with two left legs.

• Our best description of the process of mummification comes from the Greek historian Herodotus (5th century BC). He describes three types. In the most expensive treatment, priests removed all the internal organs, washed out the inside of the body with sweet oils, then packed it up with bundles of resin and natron (a type of salt). In a less expensive treatment, the body was filled with a solution that dissolved everything inside it. With the cheapest treatment, the body was just washed with a natron solution.

• Ideally, priests preserved the liver, lungs, intestines and stomach, which were all placed in vessels called Canopic jars (below), each with the head of a god who would protect the contents. The heart was mummified separately and placed back inside the body. The brains were considered unimportant – they were pulled out through the nose with a curved hook.

Funeral Rituals – Mourning

When someone died, the family played a very important role. The women acted as mourners and walked with the coffin from the place of mummification to the tomb. Sometimes there would also be professional mourners. We know that they sang sad songs as they walked, because some of these were carved onto the walls of tombs.

Mourning women throwing dust on their hair and wailing.

One of the most bitter-sweet laments comes from the tomb of King Osorkon II of the 22nd Dynasty, and it is uttered by the general in charge of his army:

I will lament for you without stopping,
for I never tire of longing for your face.
My heart is heavy with sighs when I remember
your goodness. I would rather be enriched
with the presence of my master than any
reward I could hold. I brought my master to
his city, Thebes, that sacred place that his
heart loves. May his ba (soul) reach the
place where he rests, the mansion of millions
of years! Now that my king has become a
god, may he rest content in his place once
his ba is united with the sky.

Mourning women took on the roles of the goddesses Isis and Nephthys, who lamented over the body of their brother Osiris, when he was murdered by his brother Seth. You can see two women watching over a mummy in the model funeral boat (right). The mourning of Isis and Nephthys was part of the ritual that brought Osiris back to life, and it was re-enacted at every funeral to make sure the deceased person would also come back to life.

Wooden model of a boat carrying a coffin.

The Egyptian Soul

The Egyptians believed that a person's soul took different forms with different abilities.

The *ba* had the body and wings of a bird, and a human head. It could fly out of the tomb and visit all the places a person had loved during life.

The *ka* was a person's double. It came to life in the tomb and needed to eat and drink just like a living person. It is the *ka* that we see in tomb-paintings, sitting in front of offerings of food and drink.

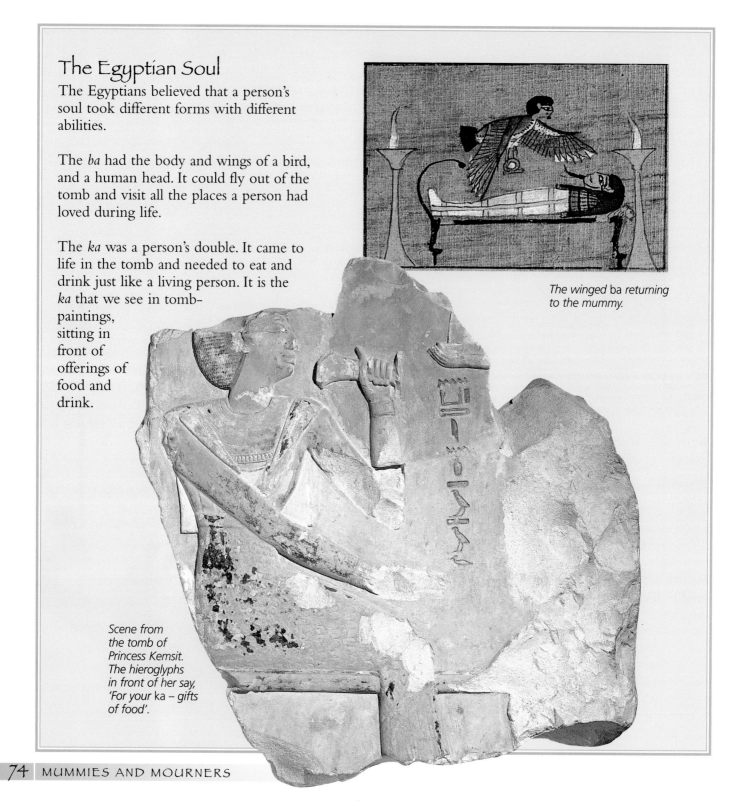

The winged ba *returning to the mummy.*

Scene from the tomb of Princess Kemsit. The hieroglyphs in front of her say, 'For your ka – gifts of food'.

The Opening of the Mouth

One of the most important ceremonies that was performed during the funeral was called 'The Opening of the Mouth' (below).

Miniature sets of the tools that were used during this ritual have survived from tombs (right). The ceremony brought the mummy of the deceased person back to life by re-awakening their senses. It was performed by a priest known as 'sem' or 'setem', who wore a leopard skin.

The ritual also used the leg of a living calf which was raised to the mummy's lips. You can see the preparation for this part of the ritual underneath the main scene, above.

Statue of a family's ancestor, once kept inside a household shrine where the family could pray to it.

Duties of Parents and Children

Children were expected to carry on the funerary cults of their parents. They cared for their tombs, and made offerings of food and prayers for the Afterlife. In return, people expected their deceased relatives to go on looking after them. Occasionally, they even wrote letters asking for help. These 'Letters to the Dead' give us glimpses of people's lives. One woman named Irty asks for protection, because a relative called Behesti is taking her furniture and staff. She asks her dead husband to summon an army of family ghosts to help her:

> Will you remain calm about this? Awaken your father, Iy, against Behesti! Raise yourself! Hurry yourself against him! … Raise yourself against them, together with your fathers and brothers and friends!

Sadly, we don't know what happened to Irty in the end.

The Afterlife

What was it like for the dead in the Afterlife? Old Kingdom texts describe the king sailing through the sky in the sun-god's boat for all eternity. By the Middle Kingdom, texts start to talk about the Field of Reeds, where a person would enjoy all the comforts of life – gentle rivers, sunny shores protected by shady trees, and plentiful harvests.

But people had to prove their worthiness before they could enter this paradise. This was done by weighing the heart in the Hall of Judgement (above).

'Weighing of the heart' scenes were painted onto papyri known as 'The Book of the Dead'. The spells collected in these papyri allowed a person to move safely through the gates of the Underworld, each of which was guarded by a fierce demon.

The 'Weighing of the Heart'. The jackal god Anubis leads the soul of the deceased towards the Scales of Justice. The dead man's heart is weighed against the Feather of Truth. The scribe-god Thoth writes down the verdict. The heart must be lighter than the feather or the man will not be allowed into the Afterlife. If it is heavier, it is eaten by the crocodile-headed monster Ammut.

Even in the Field of Reeds, there was work to be done. That is why the Egyptians invented the *shabti*. Shabtis were little servant figures inscribed with a magical formula to bring them to life when work needed to be done in the Afterlife. They were programmed with the response:

Here I am! I will do it!

A lady called Henutmehyt had four of these colourful boxes of shabti servants.

Life After Death

At the beginning of the chapter, we asked the question, why were the Egyptians so focused on their Afterlife? One answer is that they loved their life so much that they never wanted it to end. They believed that if they prepared in the right way, their souls would spend eternity in a land exactly like Egypt but with all life's hardships removed, while all the best things in life were still possible – the joys of food and drink, the pleasure of being able to move around. Even better, they would become powerful enough to solve any problem suffered by the family they loved. Does this mean that they were never afraid or anxious about leaving life? Many texts have survived that encourage people to make the most of life, precisely because what happens after death is so uncertain:

No one returns from the beyond
to tell us about their condition ...

It seems that the Egyptians were most afraid of their existence simply ending, and of their names being forgotten. Every magical ritual, every religious ceremony, all the efforts made by builders and craftsmen who prepared tombs and their furnishings, every prayer uttered by family members was designed to prevent this from happening. But as long as people visit their temples and tombs, or look at museum collections, they will never die. For the Egyptians, that is Paradise.

Scenes of the Afterlife in Nakht's Book of the Dead papyrus.

The scribe Nakht is guided by his winged soul (ba) towards his tomb, while the sun shines down on them.

Find Out More

You can find out more about many of the objects shown on these pages, and other items in the British Museum, by going to the website **www.britishmuseum.org** and clicking on 'Explore the British Museum'.

If you want to learn more about the world of the ancient Egyptians, try the books listed below. There are two separate lists for younger and for older readers.

FOR YOUNGER READERS

General Guides to Ancient Egypt

Joyce Filer (2007) *Pocket Explorer: Ancient Egypt and the Nile*, British Museum Press.

Geraldine Harris and Delia Pemberton (1999; 2005 new edition) *The Illustrated Encyclopaedia of Ancient Egypt*, British Museum Press.

Robert Morkot (2001) *The Empires of Ancient Egypt*, BBC Books

Delia Pemberton (2005) *Illustrated Atlas of Ancient Egypt*, British Museum Press.

Kings and Queens

Marcel Marée (2005) *British Museum Pocket Dictionary: Pharaohs and Queens*, British Museum Press.

Anne Millard (1998) *The New Book of Pharaohs*, Aladdin, Watts.

Hendrikje Nouwens (2007) *Tutankhamun: Ultimate Activity Book,* British Museum Press.

Officials and Scribes

Richard Parkinson (2004) *Pocket Guide to Egyptian Hieroglyphs*, British Museum Press.

Households and Families

Alison Cooper (2001) *What Families were Like – Ancient Egypt*, Hodder Wayland Press.

Builders and Craftsmen

Joyce Filer (2005) *Pyramids and People in Ancient Egypt*, British Museum Press

Soldiers and Conquerors

Anne Millard (2000) *Going to War in Ancient Egypt*, Grolier Publishing.

Mummies and Mourners

Meredith Hooper (2008) *The Tomb of Nebamun*, British Museum Press.

Delia Pemberton (2001) *Egyptian Mummies: People of the Past,* British Museum Press.

Nigel Strudwick (2004) *British Museum Pocket Dictionary: Ancient Egyptian Mummies*, British Museum Press.

FOR OLDER READERS

General Guides to Ancient Egypt

John Baines and Jaromir Malek (2000) *Cultural Atlas of Ancient Egypt*, Checkmark Books.

T.G.H. James (2005) *The British Museum Concise Introduction: Ancient Egypt*, British Museum Press.

Ian Shaw and Paul Nicholson (1995; 2008 new edition) *The British Museum Dictionary of Ancient Egypt*, British Museum Press.

Collections of Egyptian Texts

Miriam Lichtheim (1973-1980; 2006 new edition) *Ancient Egyptian Literature*, 3 volumes, University of California Press.

A.G. McDowell (1999) *Village Life in Ancient Egypt. Laundry Lists and Love Songs*, Oxford University Press.

Richard B. Parkinson (1991) *Voices from Ancient Egypt*, British Museum Press.

Richard B. Parkinson (1998) *The Tale of Sinuhe and Other*

Ancient Egyptian Poems 1940–1640 BC, Oxford University Press.

Kings and Queens
Peter A. Clayton (1994) *Chronicle of the Pharaohs*, Thames and Hudson.
Aidan Dodson and Dyan Hilton (2004) *The Complete Royal Families of Ancient Egypt*, Thames and Hudson.
Stephen Quirke (1990) *Who were the Pharaohs? A History of their Names with a List of their Cartouches*, British Museum Press.

Officials and Scribes
T.G.H. James (1984; 2006 new edition) *Pharaoh's People: Scenes from Life in Imperial Egypt*, Tauris Parke Paperbacks.
Eugene Strouhal (1992) *Life in Ancient Egypt*, Cambridge University Press.

Priests and Priestesses:
Stephen Quirke (1992) *Ancient Egyptian Religion*, British Museum Press.
Serge Sauneron (2000) *The Priests of Ancient Egypt*, Cornell University Press.
Richard H. Wilkinson (2000) *The Complete Temples of Ancient Egypt*, Thames and Hudson.

Households and Families
Rosalind M. and Jac. J. Janssen (1990) *Growing Up in Ancient Egypt*, The Rubicon Press.
Gay Robins (1993) *Women in Ancient Egypt*, British Museum Press.

Farmers and Herdsmen
Patrick F. Houlihan (1996) *The Animal World of the Pharaohs*, Thames and Hudson.
Rosalind and Jac. J Janssen (1989) *Egyptian Household Animals*, Shire Egyptology.
Hilary Wilson (1988) *Egyptian Food and Drink*, Shire Egyptology.

Builders and Craftsmen
Morris Bierbrier (1989; 1992 new edition) *The Tomb-builders of the Pharaohs*, American University in Cairo Press.
Rosalie David (1980) *The Pyramid Builders of Ancient Egypt*, Routledge.
Geoffrey Killen (1994) *Egyptian Woodworking and Furniture*, Shire Egyptology.
Richard Parkinson (2008) *The Painted Tomb-Chapel of Nebamun*, British Museum Press.
Gay Robins (2001) *Egyptian Statues*, Shire Egyptology.

Soldiers and Conquerors
Bridget McDermott (2004) *Warfare in Ancient Egypt*, Sutton Publishing.
Ian Shaw (1991) *Warfare and Weapons*, Shire Egyptology.

Musicians and Dancers
L. Manniche (1991) *Music and Musicians in Ancient Egypt*, British Museum Press.

Foreigners and Travellers
John Baines and Jaromir Malek (2000) *Cultural Atlas of Ancient Egypt*, Checkmark Books.
Piotr Bienkowski and Alan R. Millard (2000) *The British Museum Dictionary of the Ancient Near East*, British Museum Press.

Mummies and Mourners
Aidan Dodson and Salima Ikram (1998) *The Mummy in Ancient Egypt*, Thames and Hudson.
John H. Taylor (2001) *Death and the Afterlife in Ancient Egypt*, British Museum Press.

Index